About Reading Connection:

W9-API-758

Welcome to RBP Books' Connection series. Reading Connection provides students with focused practice to help reinforce and develop reading skills in areas appropriate for fifth-grade students. Reading Connection uses a variety of writing types and exercises to help build comprehension, thinking, phonics, vocabulary, language, reasoning, and other skills important to both reading and critical thinking. In accordance with NCTE (National Council of Teachers of English) standards, reading material, and exercises are grade-level appropriate and use controlled vocabulary, and clear examples and instructions on each page guide the lesson. Activities help students develop reading skills and give special attention to vocabulary development.

Dear Parents and Educators,

Thank you for choosing this Rainbow Bridge Publishing educational product to help teach your children and students. We take great pride and pleasure in becoming involved with your educational experience. Some people say that math will always be math and reading will always be reading, but we do not share that opinion. Reading, math, spelling, writing, geography, science, history, and all other subjects will always be some of life's most fulfilling adventures and should be taught with passion both at home and in the classroom. Because of this, we at Rainbow Bridge Publishing associate the greatness of learning with every product we create.

It is our mission to provide materials that not only explain, but also amaze; not only review, but also encourage; not only guide, but also lead. Every product contains clear, concise instructions, appropriate sample work, and engaging, grade-appropriate content created by classroom teachers and writers that is based on national standards to support your best educational efforts. We hope you enjoy our company's products as you embark on your adventure. Thank you for bringing us along.

Sincerely,

George Starks
Associate Publisher
Rainbow Bridge Publishing

Reading Connection™ • Grade 5
Compiled and Written by Jenie Skoy

© 2003 Rainbow Bridge Publishing. All rights reserved.

Permission to Reproduce

Illustrations
Jonathan Hallett

Visual Design and Layout
Andy Carlson, Robyn Funk, Zachary Johnson, Scott Whimpey

Publisher
Scott G. Van Leeuwen

Editorial Director
Paul Rawlins

Associate Publisher
George Starks

Copy Editors and Proofreaders
Suzie Ellison, Linda Swain, Esther Yu

Series Creator
Michele Van Leeuwen

Technology Integration
James Morris, Dante J. Orazzi

Please visit our website at
www.summerbridgeactivities.com
for supplements, additions, and corrections to this book.

First Edition 2003

For orders call 1-800-598-1441
Discounts available for quantity orders

ISBN: 1-932210-20-2

PRINTED IN THE UNITED STATES OF AMERICA
10 9 8 7 6 5 4 3 2 1

Some material comes from

Our National Parks
John Muir
Boston and New York
Houghton, Mifflin and Company, 1901

Steep Trails
John Muir
Boston and New York
Houghton, Mifflin and Company, 1918

Wilderness World of John Muir
John Muir
Boston and New York
Houghton, Mifflin and Company, 1954

How to Tell Stories to Children, and Some Stories to Tell
Sara Cone Bryant
London
George G. Harrap Company
23 Portsmouth Street Kingsway W.C.
1915

Indian Why Stories
Frank B. Linderman
Charles Scribner's Sons 1915

Table of Contents

5th Grade Suggested Reading List

Adoff, Arnold
Sports Pages

Aiken, Joan
The Wolves of Willoughby Chase

Alexander, Lloyd
The Castle of Llyr
Taran Wanderer
Black Cauldron

Babbitt, Natalie
Tuck Everlasting

Banks, Lynne Reid
The Adventures of King Midas
Indian in the Cupboard

Bawden, Nina
Humbug

Burnett, Frances Hodgson
The Secret Garden

Butterworth, Oliver
Enormous Egg

Cassedy, Sylvia
Behind the Attic Wall

Clark, Ann Nolan
Secret of the Andes

Creech, Sharon
Love That Dog

Cruise, Beth
Saved by the Bell series

Curtis, Christopher Paul
Bud, Not Buddy

Dahl, Roald
Matilda
James and the Giant Peach
The Witches
The BFG

De Angeli, Marguerite
The Door in the Wall

DiCamillo, Kate
Because of Winn-Dixie

Drucker, Malka
Jacob's Rescue

Estes, Eleanor Ruth
The Hundred Dresses

Ferguson, Alane
Cricket and the Crackerbox Kid

Fitzhugh, Louise
Harriet the Spy

Fleischman, Paul
I Am Phoenix
Joyful Noise

Garland, Sherry and
Trina Schart Hyman
Children of the Dragon:
Selected Tales from Vietnam

George, Jean Craighead
My Side of the Mountain
Julie of the Wolves

Grahame, Kenneth
Wind in the Willows

Hahn, Mary Downing
Wait Till Helen Comes

Henry, Marguerite
King of the Wind

Horvath, Polly
The Trolls

Irving, Washington
Legend of Sleepy Hollow

Juster, Norton
The Phantom Tollbooth

L'Engle, Madeleine
A Wrinkle in Time

Lowry, Lois
Number the Stars

Moody, Ralph
Little Britches: Father and I Were
Ranchers

O'Dell, Scott
Island of the Blue Dolphins

Park, Barbara
Operation: Dump the Chump
Skinnybones

Pinkwater, Daniel
Lizard Music

Prelutsky, Jack
Tyrannosaurus Was a Beast

Raskin, Ellen
The Westing Game

Rawls, Wilson
Where the Red Fern Grows
Summer of the Monkeys

Roberts, Willo Davis
The Pet-Sitting Peril

Ruckman, Ivy
Night of the Twisters

Seredy, Kate
The White Stag

Smith, Robert Kimmel
The War with Grandpa

Sperry, Armstrong
Call It Courage

Taylor, Sydney
All-of-a-Kind Family

Terban, Marvin
Hey, Hay! A Wagonful of Funny
Homonym Riddles

Tolkien, J.R.R.
The Hobbit
Lord of the Rings

Travers, P.L.
Mary Poppins

Twohill, Maggie
Valentine Frankenstein

Ullman, James Ramsey
Banner in the Sky

Weston, Carol
The Diary of Melanie Martin

Willard, Nancy
A Visit to William Blake's Inn

Winthrop, Elizabeth
The Castle in the Attic
The Battle for the Castle

Wyss, Johann David
The Swiss Family Robinson

Yep, Laurence
Dragonwings

Frozen in Time: Archeologists Find Ancient Ice Woman

This Snow White needed more than a kiss from a handsome prince to wake her up!

For 2,400 years the body of a Siberian woman lay under the plains of the Ukok Plateau in Russia, frozen in a huge ice cube. The ice kept her body preserved until 1994, when a team of archeologists carefully excavated the grave.

What the scientists found as the ice melted tells an amazing story. The archeologists named the woman the Lady. She had been a member of the Pazyryk culture. The Pazyryk people were hunters, sheepherders, and artists who lived from the sixth to the second century B.C. The grave was full of amazing finds, including six horses. The archeologists believe the woman owned the horses. They think the horses were killed during the Lady's funeral, then lowered into her grave.

Imagine how careful you would be if you were digging for treasure that was 2,400 years old. Archeologists uncovered the woman slowly so they wouldn't damage anything they found. When they reached the Lady's coffin, they pulled out six bronze nails from the lid. Inside they found another two feet of ice. It took three days to melt through it by pouring in cupfuls of hot water. The melting ice revealed a beautiful ancient woman. First, they saw her jawbone with flesh that looked like leather still on it. Next, the shoulder came into view. On her shoulder was a beautiful blue tattoo of a mystical creature. She had another tattoo on her thumb, and another on her wrist that looked like a deer.

The Lady was 5'6" tall, which would have been tall for her time. She had beads wrapped around her wrists and a tall, decorated headdress on her head. She was wrapped in animal fur and dressed in a long robe.

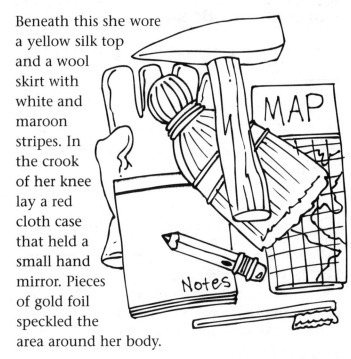

Beneath this she wore a yellow silk top and a wool skirt with white and maroon stripes. In the crook of her knee lay a red cloth case that held a small hand mirror. Pieces of gold foil speckled the area around her body.

Beside the woman stood a table. It held a meal of mutton (sheep) and a slab of horse meat with a bronze knife still sticking out of it. It was a tradition to place a meal with the person being buried. The archeologists also found a stone dish with coriander seeds in it. Coriander was an herb that the Pazyryk people thought would help the dead person journey from life to the afterlife.

The things the archeologists found fit together like the pieces of a puzzle, which made a picture of what life was like for the ancient ice woman. Archeologists even looked at the food inside the horses' stomachs to see what clues they might find. They found half-digested pine needles, grass, and twigs, which told them that the Lady's funeral had been held in the spring.

Archeologists were able to discover that the Lady died of natural causes at about the age of 25. The whole community took part in her funeral, surrounding her body with all kinds of treasures. Each treasure held a secret that whispered to archeologists, telling them just who this ancient woman was.

© RBP Books   www.summerbridgeactivities.com   Reading Connection—Grade 5—RBP0202

Uncovering Ideas

1. What did archeologists do to melt the ice around the woman?

   _____

   _____

   What do you think about the way they did this?

   _____

   _____

   _____

2. In your opinion, what are the three most interesting things that archeologists found in the Lady's burial chamber?

   _____

   _____

   _____

Connecting to Life

1. What does this story remind you of?

   _____

   _____

2. Imagine you are an archeologist and have the chance to go on a dig to discover something. What kind of discovery would you like to make?

   _____

   _____

   _____

3. Every piece of writing has a purpose. What do you think the purpose of this story is?

   _____

   _____

   _____

Reading Skills Builder

Match the kind of writing with the purpose of the writing.

_____ newspaper article about the war in Iraq

_____ book about how to collect stamps

_____ comic book

_____ phone book

_____ Internet pop up advertisement

_____ *The Lord of the Rings*

_____ a biography about a movie star

  A. explains how to do something
  B. entertains you
  C. gives an opinion about something
  D. gives you directions
  E. gets you to buy something
  F. gives you information
  G. tells a story

Word Work

Words are made up of parts. Many parts of words that you use every day have Latin and Greek meanings. An example of this is the word *bicycle*. *Bi* means "two" and *cycle* means "wheel" or "circle." Put together, *bi + cycle*, means "two wheels."

If the word part comes at the beginning, it's called a **prefix**. If it comes at the end, it's a **suffix**. *Archeologist* is made up of two word parts—*arch + ologist*.

1. What are some other words that being with the prefix **arch-**?

   _____

   _____

2. Look at what the words you wrote down have in common. Can you guess what the prefix **arch-** means?

   _____

How to Read Like an Archeologist

What do reading and digging for treasure have in common?

Reading is like searching for hidden archeological treasures. There's a story waiting in the pages you hold in your hands. There are treasures in the words that flash in front of your eyes. Is there a word you don't know or a paragraph that is hard to understand? Just like an archeologist, you look for clues to give you the answer. As you read each page, you dig a little deeper, getting closer to the treasure. Here are some rules to help you dig.

The first rule is to have an idea of what you are looking for. Archeologists wouldn't look for a pyramid in Antarctica, just like you wouldn't expect to find out how to build a go-cart in a book about the African mud frog. Each story you read was written for a purpose. Ask yourself these questions: What is the purpose of this story? Is it to teach me how to do something, to convince me, or just to make me laugh?

Sometimes it helps to ask questions while you read, just like archeologists begin their work with questions about what they will find. After they discover a burial chamber, archeologists may ask questions like these: Where did this person come from? How did she die? How did she live? The answers come slowly and sometimes in strange ways. Do you remember how archeologists found out what time of year the ancient ice lady died?

The next rule for reading is to pay attention to the small details in the story that may tell you what will happen next. In many stories, the author may give you clues about what will happen; this is called **foreshadowing**.

The third rule is to take your time when you read. Any good archeologist knows that if they rush to uncover something, they may ruin an ancient treasure along the way. Maybe you think smart readers read quickly. But smart readers go slowly so they won't miss anything. They know that careful reading helps them understand the story.

The last idea is to have fun. Sometimes reading seems fun and exciting, but, like anything else, it can also be hard work. How fun do you think it is to stand over an ancient coffin for three days and pour cups of water over a frozen mummy? But being patient is part of making a discovery. You can't expect every story you read to be exciting all the time. But you never know what treasure you might find in the end!

Whether you are going on an adventure to dig up ancient bones or just reading a new story, remember:

Some basic rules before you begin "The Dig"

1. Have an idea of what you are looking for.

2. Ask questions along the way.

3. Follow your intuition (feelings or ideas that send you in a certain direction).

4. Train your eye to see small things and pay attention to everything surrounding the main find.

5. Be open to surprises. Don't be so focused on what you "want" to find that you cannot see what is really there.

6. Take your time; you might miss something important.

7. Have fun!

Uncovering Ideas

1. According to the story, what are three ways reading is like digging for treasure?

   _____

   _____

   _____

2. Think about the last book or story you read. On a scale from 1 to 5, how hard was this story to read?

   easy   **difficult**

   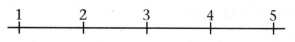

   1   2   3   4   5

3. Write down three other stories or books that you've read recently. Put them on the scale.

   _____

   _____

   _____

4. Make a list of ten different things you read every day. Include the back of the cereal box, street signs, etc.

   _____

   _____

   _____

   _____

Reading Skills Builder

When the author compares reading to digging for treasures, she is using a **metaphor**. A metaphor compares two different things. Here are a few metaphors written by students:

Examples:

   Homework is a sweaty sock: it stinks!

   People are mirrors; you can see yourself in them.

   Sleep is a stone, quiet and still.

Write your own metaphor by comparing two different things.

1. Sleep is _____

2. Life is _____

3. Anger is a _____

4. Happiness is _____

5. Friendship is_____

Word Work

Read this poem and answer the questions.

> **Fog**
> by Carl Sandburg
>
> The fog comes
> On little cat feet.
>
> It sits looking
> Over harbor and city
> On silent haunches
> And then moves on.

1. How does the fog sit?

   _____

2. Where does the fog look?

   _____

3. What does the fog do at the end of the poem?

   _____

   _____

4. What does the poet compare the fog to?

   _____

The Hero of Harlem

Adapted from Sara Cone Bryant, *How to Tell Stories to Children, and Some Stories to Tell*

Do you think you can make a difference in the world?

Holland is a little country across the ocean where much of the ground is lower than the level of the sea, instead of higher. Of course, this means the water would run in and cover the land and houses if something didn't keep it out. So over the centuries, the people built thick walls all around the country to keep the sea out. These walls are called dikes, and they are as wide as a road. Everything the people of Holland have built depends on those walls. Even the children know that damage to one of the walls is a terrible thing.

Hans was a child who lived in Holland long ago, in a small town called Harlem. One day he took his little brother out to play. They went a long way out of the town until they came to a place where there were no houses, only flowers and green fields. Hans climbed up on the dike and sat down to watch the sea while his little brother was playing at the foot of the bank.

Suddenly his little brother called out, "Look at this funny little hole! It bubbles!"

"Hole?" said Hans. "Where?"

"Here in the bank," said his little brother. "There's water in it."

"What?" said Hans. He slid down as fast as he could to where his brother was playing. There was the tiniest little hole in the bank. Just an airhole. A drop of water bubbled slowly through.

"It is a hole in the dike!" Hans cried. "What do we do?"

He looked round; there wasn't a person or a house in sight. He looked at the hole where the little drops oozed steadily through. He knew the little hole would get bigger and bigger. All the water needed was a chance, and soon enough it would come bursting through. If they ran for

help, they might be too late. The town was too far away. Hans looked down again. The hole was larger now, and the water was trickling in a tiny stream.

Almost without thinking, Hans stuck his forefinger into the hole until it fit tight. Then he told his little brother to run.

"You've got to run to town and warn them that there's a hole in the dike. Tell them I will keep it stopped till they get here."

His little brother knew by the look on Hans's face that something was very wrong, and he started for the town as fast as he could run. Hans knelt with his finger in the hole, watching his brother grow smaller and smaller as he got farther away. Soon he was as small as a chicken; then he was only a speck; then he was out of sight. Hans was alone, his finger tight in the bank.

He could hear the water slapping on the stones, and deep down under the slapping was the gurgling, rumbling sound of the entire ocean on the other side of the dike.

It seemed very near.   *(to be continued)*

www.summerbridgeactivities.com   Reading Connection—Grade 5—RBP0202

Uncovering Ideas

1. Why is there a wall around the country?

_____

_____

2. Why did Hans put his finger in the hole in the wall?

_____

_____

3. What did Hans tell his little brother to do?

_____

_____

Connecting to Life

1. The story talks about a discovery that a boy made when he was playing with his brother. Think about a discovery you have made while you were hanging out with friends. In the box below, draw a picture to show what you discovered.

```



```

Reading Skills Builder

Read the information below and answer the questions.

The Moonbeam Film Festival presents five days of independent films in the heart of the Sawtooth Mountains. Along with the films, there will be an art show, a street dance with fireworks, and a rodeo. For more information, call the Stanley City Council or contact us at *www.moonbeamfilmsidaho.com*.

1. Besides watching films, what else can you do during the Moonbeam Film Festival?

_____

_____

2. List two places you can go to find more information about the film festival.

_____

_____

Word Work

Dialogue in a story is when people talk back and forth. You can tell an author is using dialogue when the words are in quotation marks:

"Look at this funny little hole, it bubbles!"

"Hole?" said Hans. "Where?"

Write your own dialogue between animals talking. Be sure to put quotes around what each animal says.

Giraffe said to the elephant, _____

Elephant said to the giraffe,_____

Giraffe said back, _____

All of a sudden something strange happened. (What happened?) _____

_____

Elephant said, _____

Giraffe said, _____

The moral of this story is: _____

Have you ever been so afraid you wanted to run?

For a long time after his brother had disappeared from sight, Hans knelt by the dike. His hand began to go numb. He rubbed it with the other hand, but it grew colder and number by the minute. He looked into the distance to see if the townspeople were coming, but the road was empty as far as he could see.

The cold began creeping up his arm. First he felt it in his wrist. Then it spread along his forearm up to his elbow. He could feel it crawling like a bug up to his shoulder. It was so cold! Then his arm began to ache. Like the cold, a cramp started in his finger and spread to his palm. It worked its way up to his shoulder and into his neck. Hans peered up toward the sky where wispy gray clouds had blocked the sun. It seemed as if hours had gone by since his brother had left. He stared hard down the road again, straining to see somebody, anybody, but there was no one. Then he leaned against the wall of the dike to rest his shoulder.

As his ear touched the dike, he seemed to hear the voice of the ocean murmuring. It seemed to say, "I am the great sea. No one can stand against me. You are only a little boy. Do you think you can keep me out? Do you think you can stop me? Beware, boy. Beware!"

Hans's heart knocked against his chest. Where was everybody? Why hadn't they come?

The water seemed to beat more heavily against the wall, and the sea began to murmur again.

"I will come through; I will come through. I will get you—run, run before I burst through!"

Hans began to pull his finger from the dike. He had to run! He had to run before the sea broke through.

He thought of the sea bursting though the dike. He could imagine a great flood spreading far out over the land. As the dike crumbled, the water would rush over the fields and tumble down the road. Its great white fingers of foam would stretch toward the town, churning everything in its path. The fingers would crush the school and the church and his home.

As he thought of it, he gritted his teeth and shoved his finger into the dike tighter than ever.

"You will not come through," he whispered. "I will not run."

At that moment, he heard a far-off shout. Far in the distance, he saw a black speck along the road. The townspeople were coming—at last they were coming! They were coming quickly, and as they came nearer, he could make out his own father as well as neighbors among the group. They carried pickaxes and shovels. "We're coming!" they shouted as they ran. "Hold on, we're coming!"

It seemed like only a moment before the crowd was there. When they saw Hans, with his face gone pale and his finger wedged tight into the dike, they gave a cheer. They hoisted him onto their shoulders like a soldier who was coming home from a war. Once the dike was fixed, they put him back on their shoulders and carried him like that all the way to town—their hero. And to this day, the people of Holland tell the story of Hans, the boy who saved Harlem.

Uncovering Ideas

1. The **theme** of a story is what a story teaches. What is one of the themes in this story?

   _____

   _____

2. Think about **cause** and **effect**. If Hans had not stopped the water with his finger, what do you think would have happened?

   _____

   _____

Connecting to Life

1. Think about another story you've read, or a movie you watched, where one person helped many people by doing something simple. What did the person do? What was the result?

   _____

   _____

2. How can you make a difference by something small that you do?

   _____

   _____

Reading Skills Builder

Read the following story and answer the questions below.

How to Convince Your Little Sister to Clean Your Room
By Blake Faker

If your sister loves to find hidden treasures, tell her to pretend your room is a jungle and you are looking for the mysterious silver goblet. (You can use a mug covered with tinfoil.) Bury the goblet in a pile of clothes. Tell her she must put the clothes back in your drawers as she searches.

If that doesn't work, offer to baby-sit her cat for a day. If she doesn't trust you with her cat, try the "sick" approach. Lie on your bed and groan loudly enough for her to hear. When she comes in, tell her how bad you feel, start shaking, and fake a fever. Tell her you wish you could clean your room. She may just do it for you.

1. List the three ways the author says you can convince your sister to clean your room.

   _____

   _____

   _____

2. How does he suggest you make a mysterious silver goblet?

   _____

   _____

3. Do you think the author of this story will be able to convince his sister to clean his room? Why or why not?

   _____

   _____

Word Work

Personification is when writers give human qualities to a non-living thing. An example of this is when the sea talks to Hans as though it were alive. Personify (or give life to) one of the following things by creating a conversation between them.

What would a:

1. Pencil say to a hand?

2. Carpet say to a foot?

3. Basketball say to a basketball player?

4. Skateboard say to a skateboarder?

   _____

   _____

   _____

   _____

Devil's Spit

By Jenie Skoy

What have you discovered about yourself through your own experiences?

Standing knee deep in the cold rapids, I watched the river carry leaves, sticks, and a few bird feathers along. It felt like the river wanted to carry me along, too.

"Let go of the tree branch," Jim said.

Jim was squatting on a big rock in the middle of the river upstream. He was convincing me that I was as brave as he was. When I was in the third grade, he told me I could jump off the roof of our shed and land straight on my feet, but I landed straight on something else. Jim carried me around for a few days, till I could walk without screaming out in pain.

Jim was big. His hands were huge and freckled, and his fingernails sprouted faster than Mom could cut 'em. He was built lanky and wore a head full of thick, honey blonde hair that stuck out in three different directions when he woke up in the morning.

He didn't bother brushing his hair before we went to the river.

I loosened my grip on the branch and tried balancing myself in the river's current. It was cold like a winter night with no covers, and strong like a wind sweeping over a plain; it wanted to pick me up and take me someplace else.

Jim was yelling out to me, cheering me on like he had when I was teetering on top of that old roof. Jim always knew that I could do it. I fought the water to make it to him upstream. My face was beginning to burn red, but the sun made it a perfect day to go river climbing—that's what Jim

called it. But the water seemed colder than usual, and the river acted hungry, like it wanted to eat me alive. I stubbed my toe, but I couldn't feel it because I was numb from my knees down. I was getting tired, and I guess Jim could tell because he told me to hurry it up.

"Quit being a girl, Jess, and move faster," Jim said.

I hated it when Jim called me a girl, even though I was one. The guys at school never dared call me a girl; they knew I wasn't a sissy like the others, wearing bows and lace and making a fuss if they got a bit of dirt on them. I'd never be like them. I fixed a mean look to my face, squinted my eyes, and clenched my teeth. I made my hands into two fists and pushed my body through the water towards Jim.

As I stepped, a sharp rock on the bottom bit into my ankle, sending a shot of pain up my leg right to my belly button. I let out a scream and lost my balance, tumbling into the freezing current sideways. I gave up fighting and let the river take me for a ride.

"Where are you going now?" Jim yelled out to me. "Come on, get up and try it again!"

I ignored him for a minute and floated to the side of the river, taking hold of another tree branch.

(to be continued)

© RBP Books   www.summerbridgeactivities.com   Reading Connection—Grade 5—RBP0202

Uncovering Ideas

1. What is the setting in the first part of this story? What are they doing?

   _____

   _____

   _____

2. Find a part in the story that tells what kind of relationship Jess and Jim have. Do they get along or not?

   _____

   _____

   _____

3. The narrator is the person telling the story. Who is the narrator?

   _____

   Circle the best answer about the narrator.
   a. She doesn't like to go outside.
   b. She dislikes her brother.
   c. She tries to be a tomboy.
   d. She is older than Jim.

4. Why doesn't Jess want people to call her a girl?

   _____

Connecting to Life

1. Many stories are based on real places and things that happened. "Devil's Spit" is an example of a story based on truth; the author grew up by the Snake River in a small Idaho town. She and her family used to play in the river all summer. Which parts of the story do you think are true, and which parts are made up?

   True   Made up

   _____   _____

   _____   _____

   _____   _____

2. On a separate sheet of paper, write about an adventure you had outside with family or friends.

Reading Skills Builder

Write three **synonyms** for each word below. Synonyms are words, like *drink* and *beverage*, that have the same meaning.

feminine

_____   _____   _____

masculine

_____   _____   _____

Word Work

Masculine and Feminine Words

Change all the masculine words into feminine ones and rewrite the sentences.

1. The actress did a great job playing the bride of a monster.

   The actor did a great job playing the

   groom of a monster.

2. The queen's son is the hero of the story.

   _____

   _____

3. My nephew asked me to read him a story about the Princess and the Pea.

   _____

   _____

4. The waiter took the meal to the hungry man.

   _____

   _____

5. The old man went searching for the ram.

   _____

   _____

Devil's Spit (continued)

By Jenie Skoy

I pulled my body out of the water and lay like a wet rat on the riverbank, inviting the sun to warm my bones. Then I found an easier way upstream. I limped barefoot on a mass of old volcanic rocks and stranded river sticks to where Jim lay on the rock.

Jim looked asleep; he'd given up on me. I had an idea to sneak up and splash him before he knew what was coming, so I slid into the water, but before I could get to him, Jim let out some kind of war cry and jumped to his feet, stretching his fingers to the sky.

"HIIIEEEEEE IAHHH OWWEEE!" he yelled to the trees and fish, making the hair on my arms stand straight up.

"Hey, little sister," he said, looking down at me still crouched in the river. Jim helped me up. I was careful with my ankle. It still hurt from twisting it, but I bit my tongue and didn't show it.

My wet clothes stuck to my body and the warm rock felt good against my back. I imagined standing under Devil's Spit, a sun-warmed waterfall that wound through a craggy rock wall that looked like the face of the devil himself. "I don't think I'm gonna make it up to Devil's Spit today," I said, thinking how far it was to the spot that Jim had discovered years ago.

"Ah Jess, you can make it." Jim said. "Do you need a little shove?" Then he rolled me into the river like a log.

I didn't tell Jim my foot was still hurting; I figured he would just tell me to stop being a sissy. I was the only little brother he had, even though I was his sister. I made it to the riverbank and climbed out on the dry rocks and over the mossy ones to where Jim was yodeling under the falls.

"You made it, Sis," Jim hollered over the sound of the rushing water. I sat down a ways from the falls on a slimy rock to catch my breath. The wet air felt good in my mouth and nose. Jim beckoned to me, but I didn't dare stand straight under the falls.

I watched Jim playing in Devil's Spit. He was weaving back and forth through the rocks on the wall beside the waterfall like a snake. He and the water were dancing: turning, laughing, and falling, then getting up again. I wished I was as brave as he was. But he was standing too close to the falls.

"Jim!" I yelled to warn him.

Jim looked over at me, grinned, and started to say something. Then he began to slip on the slick, scummy rocks. He reached out, trying to balance himself, but there was nothing to hold him up.

I watched Jim's legs buckle under him, and before I knew it, the rush of water pushed him down the mountain of bulging rocks. I saw the blur of his body under the surging water as Devil's Spit forced him down the falls!

(to be continued)

www.summerbridgeactivities.com   Reading Connection—Grade 5—RBP0202

Uncovering Ideas

1. Draw the main ideas or plot of the story. Write the main idea in each picture box.

Connecting to Life

1. Choose one character from the story and compare that person with someone you know. Explain how they are alike and different. Include examples.

_____

_____

_____

_____

2. Think of a time when you had a problem that needed to be solved or helped someone who had been hurt. What did you do?

_____

_____

_____

Reading Skills Builder

Search for the perfect e-card.

Section A—Birthday
Funny   Belated   For Her   For Him

Section B—For Friends
Hello   Missing You   Thank You   Get Well
I'm Sorry   Congratulations   Sympathy

Section C—Events and Occasions
Anniversary   Invitations   Graduation
Weddings   New Baby

Section D—Holidays
Fourth of July   Summer
Groundhog Day   Passover

1. Under what section and topic would you find a card for your sister who is sick?

_____

2. Under what section and topic would you find a card for a friend who's getting married?

_____

3. Under what section and topic would you look for a Happy Fourth of July e-card?

_____

Word Work

Use these words in the sentences below:

there	they're	their

1. Bob, will you put my groceries over _____?

2. _____ going to the mall to buy a new outfit.

3. The teacher told them to put _____ book bags against the wall.

By Jenie Skoy

Jim's body looked like it was all arms and legs where it lay at the bottom of the rocks.

I was beside Jim without thinking; crying, praying, asking him if he was all right, holding his bruised-up face in my hands. I watched him try to move, then yelp like a hurt puppy dog. He opened his eyes and looked past me like I wasn't there, then closed them and opened them again.

"Jess, help me," he managed to say, looking at me like I was his angel of mercy.

I talked to Jim a bit to make sure he was all there. I tore off a piece of my shirt, and put it to his bleeding forehead, then helped him to a dry spot on the grass.

He looked so small, not like the Jim I knew. I didn't want to leave him there, but I knew I needed to get some help. I arranged Jim to make him as comfortable as possible, then jumped back into the river. My feet slid on the rocks, and the river tripped me, pushing me deep under the current. I came up cold and gasping for air. I didn't care; I just kept moving.

A cloud passed over the sun as I got out of the river, and I ran through the woods in a deep shadow. I was shivering and praying and staggering wildly. It wasn't far to home, but it seemed like I'd never get there. Why did I have to hurt my ankle? Why couldn't I run faster? The path through the forest looked blurry to me through my tears. I tripped a few times into the dirt and branches, standing up with scraped legs and my hands stung by sharp pine needles. I recognized my house through the woods, and I don't know how, but I finally made it there. I

ran in, crying to my parents about Jim. Mom called an ambulance. Dad picked me up and carried me while I led him to where Jim was lying over by Devil's Spit.

The next day, I woke up early, put on the jeans that I wear to the river, and went to wake up Jim. Halfway to his room, I felt a sharp pain in my foot; then I remembered my twisted ankle and what had happened at the river the day before. In my head, I saw Jim's body at the bottom of Devil's Spit. I opened the door to his room and limped fearfully to the side of his bed.

The sun was making its way through the window and fell across a sunburned body wrapped up in a blanket on the bed. Sitting on the edge of his bed, I touched Jim's bandaged forehead and put my face near his, letting my tears fall down his bruised cheek. As I cried, my whole body began to shake.

I never loved a thing more than the feel of Jim's warm breath on my cheek. I kept my face by his for many minutes and stared at his chest rising up and down. I felt like I belonged, sitting alone beside Jim on his bed. Sometimes in crowds of people, I felt alone, like everyone was too inside themselves to notice me. But Jim always included me, and looking down, I could see that I had made a difference in his life.

Jim groaned as he moved his body a little, and then he opened his eyes.

"That's my girl, Jess," he said suddenly, looking straight at me. "That's my girl."

www.summerbridgeactivities.com

Uncovering Ideas

1. How did Jess help her brother Jim?

   _____

   _____

   _____

2. What was Jess thinking about as she ran to get help?
   a. How hungry she was.
   b. She wished that she could run faster.
   c. She knew first aid.
   d. How angry her dad would be that they were late.

3. What do you think Jess discovered about herself through this experience?

   _____

   _____

   _____

Connecting to Life

1. Think about a time you learned an important lesson through a hard experience. What was the lesson?

   _____

   _____

   _____

Word Work

Circle the correct spelling of the word.

1. butterfly, butterflie
2. garbage, garbege
3. before, befour
4. nephew, nefew
5. chain, chane
6. scard, scared
7. butter, buter
8. chiken, chicken

Reading Skills Builder

Materials Needed for Star Picture Frame:

   6 Popsicle sticks   glue or glue gun
   paint or markers   photo

Steps:

1. Glue three Popsicle sticks into a triangle.

2. Glue the other three Popsicle sticks into a triangle (you should have two triangles).

3. Lay one triangle on top of the other triangle to form a star.

4. Glue together.

5. Trim your photo to fit inside the star and glue into place.

6. Attach a ribbon or yarn to the top to hang it.

Answer the questions below:

1. Name two materials that you will need for this project.

   _____

   _____

2. What can you do after you glue the photo?

   _____

   _____

3. In the space below, draw pictures to show how to do the first three steps.

Discovering the Truth of History: What Really Happened 100 Years Ago?

By Joseph Soderborg

Should you believe everything you read in a history book?

Many people think we can easily know the past, but history is not always what it seems. Let's pretend your favorite basketball team is the Houston Rockets. Say they just played an unbelievable championship game against the Los Angeles Lakers. Let's also pretend that you missed the game. You know the Rockets won, but you want to find out why they won. When you ask your friends about the game, they each tell you different versions of the story.

During overtime, the referees called a controversial foul that changed how the game ended. One of your friends says: "The Lakers were robbed. They would have won the game if it wasn't for that bogus foul!"

Other friends argue that the foul was a good call. They all agree with the referees and say that the Rockets rule! The debate goes on and on, with both sides mixing in their opinions about what they saw.

You decide to check the newspapers for the real story. At the library you look at papers from both Houston and Los Angeles, but even they print stories that disagree. Both sides sound good, but both sides can't be telling the whole truth. Even the instant replay is not very clear. The Rockets won, but you have to rely on someone's opinion of what happened to know why they won.

In this modern example, you can at least watch a videotape of the game or talk to people who were there to discover some of the facts about the game for yourself. But what about a game played a hundred years ago? You'd have to rely on written things like newspaper articles from that time, or maybe a diary kept by one of the players. Historians look at evidence like this to help piece together the puzzle of a historical event. But many of these events are much more complicated than the outcome of a basketball game. Just think of how many different opinions there would be about the Industrial Revolution or World War II.

History is not simply the facts. History is often what historians tell us about the facts. In the end, history can be defined as a "best guess." When we try to look at history, it's almost as though we are looking through a muddy window. We have to decide what happened based on what we can't see clearly. We cannot know because we were not there.

www.summerbridgeactivities.com   Reading Connection—Grade 5—RBP0202

Uncovering Ideas

1. In what ways are history and learning about a basketball game you didn't attend alike?

   _____

   _____

   _____

2. What does the author want readers to understand?

   _____

   _____

3. Do you agree with the author about his idea of what history is? Why or why not?

   _____

   _____

   _____

4. The story mentioned newspaper articles and diaries as ways to find out about the past. What are some other ways?

   _____

   _____

Connecting to Life

1. Imagine you found a time machine and were able to go back to witness an event in history. What event would you want to see and why?

   _____

   _____

   _____

   _____

2. On another sheet of paper, write a letter to a famous person asking questions about what it was like to live when he or she did.

Reading Skills Builder

Sometimes discovering what happened in the past is like solving a riddle. Come up with your best guess to solve the riddles below:

1. The more you take, the more you leave behind. What are they?

   _____

2. What has eyes yet cannot see? (This has three answers.)

   _____

3. Black within and red without. Four corners round about. What am I?

   _____

4. Nearly bright as the sun, sometimes dark as space. Like a pearl on black velvet, with diamonds twinkling in a case. What am I?

   _____

5. Take off my skin, I won't cry, but you will, what am I?

   _____

6. If you have it, you want to share it. If you share it, you don't have it. What am I?

   _____

Word Work

Spell the \k\ sound with *ch*.

1. She sings in the ___ ___ oir.

2. My favorite holiday is ___ ___ ristmas.

3. My hair turns green because of the swimming pool's ___ ___ lorine.

4. My car needs to be fixed by the me ___ ___ anic.

5. Jem is one of the main ___ ___ aracters in the book *To Kill a Mockingbird*.

Stories of Immigration: The Truth about Angel Island

By Joseph Soderborg

Do you know what country your ancestors came from?

In 1882 Congress passed a law called the Chinese **Exclusionary** Act. It was passed to keep Chinese people from coming to America. For years Chinese workers had come as merchants or to work in mines. They had helped build the railroads in the West. But some Americans were afraid that the Chinese would take jobs and cause trouble. The law passed in 1882 made it harder for Chinese to enter the country. No other people faced **discrimination** like the Chinese. They were not even allowed to be citizens until the Supreme Court said that anyone born in America was a citizen. This was important because families of citizens could **immigrate** despite the law.

At this time, there was a huge Chinatown in San Francisco. Thousands of Chinese had gone there before the law was passed. But in 1906, the San Francisco earthquake and the fire it caused destroyed much of the city. When Chinatown burned, so did the **citizenship** records. The U.S. government did not know which Chinese coming to America were related to citizens and which were not. The ones who were related would be able to stay. The ones who weren't would have to go back to China.

In 1910, the government opened a station for immigrants on Angel Island in San Francisco **Harbor**. Chinese immigrants had to wait there until they could prove they had a relative who was a citizen. Some people spent months or even years waiting to tell their story. Some told their stories through poetry that they carved on the walls of the wooden **barracks** where they stayed.

More than 250,000 Chinese immigrants, as well as people from other Asian countries and South America, came through Angel Island. Today it is a state park with bike trails, hiking trails, camping spots, and boats. The barracks where immigrants lived are a historic site. The poetry they carved there has been translated into English.

The Chinese Exclusionary Act was done away with in 1943.

www.summerbridgeactivities.com   Reading Connection—Grade 5—RBP0202

Uncovering Ideas

1. Why did the American government keep Chinese immigrants at Angel Island?

   _____
   _____
   _____
   _____

2. What caused the fire in San Francisco, and what was the result of the fire?

   _____
   _____
   _____
   _____
   _____

3. What did the Chinese Exclusionary Act do?

   _____
   _____
   _____
   _____

Connecting to Life

1. How do you feel after reading about how Chinese people were treated during this time in history?

   _____
   _____
   _____
   _____

2. What do you think would have been a better solution?

   _____
   _____
   _____
   _____

Reading Skills Builder

Number which order you would find these words in the dictionary:

_____ fearless

_____ farming

_____ frantic

_____ fingernail

_____ fantastic

Word Work

Angel Island Crossword Puzzle

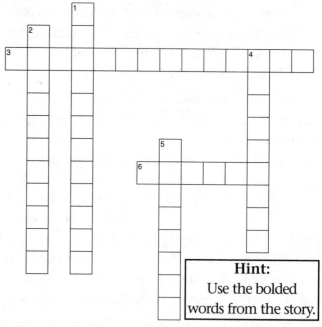

Hint:
Use the bolded words from the story.

Across

3. unfair treatment

6. a place along the ocean where ships come

Down

1. excluding someone, or keeping them from doing something

2. official right to belong as a member of a country

4. coming to a new country from another one

5. a building that many people lived in

Poems from Angel Island

If possible, find three other people to read this skit about Angel Island with you.

Tour Guide: Welcome to the Angel Island Immigration Center. Surrounding you in this small wooden barracks is a record of the people who stayed here many years ago, from 1910 to 1940. What do you see on this wall?

Student: Something has been carved into the wood, and it's in another language.

Tour Guide: That's right. The writing is Chinese. What do you think it says?

Student: We used to write on the walls of our cabin during camp. We'd write the names of the people we had a crush on and things like that.

Tour Guide: What is written on this wall is a little different. Let's look closely and ask our Chinese translators, Lui and Hai, to help us figure out what it says.

Lui: "I took a raft and sailed the seas."

Hai: "Rising early at dawn with the stars above my head."

Lui: "Traveling deep into the night, the moon my companion."

Lui and Hai: "Who would have known my trip would have been full of rain and snow?"

Tour Guide: Many Chinese people left their homes and sailed to America, but when they got here, they had to wait to become citizens. They stayed in these small wooden barracks.

Student: Why did they write on the walls?

Tour Guide: Imagine you were forced to live in a place like this. How would you feel?

Student: I would feel angry, or maybe sad.

Tour Guide: Here are some other examples from poems carved into the wall. They tell us more about how the Chinese people felt.

Lui: "I have walked to the very edge of the earth."

Hai: "A dusty, windy journey."

Lui: "I'm worn out.

"Who can save me? I am like a fish out of water."

Lui and Hai: "I worry for my parents, my wife, and my boy. Do they have enough firewood and rice?"

Lui: "We are kept in a dark, filthy room."

Hai: "Who would think that my joy would turn into sorrow?"

Lui: "Cruel treatment, not one breath of air."

Lui and Hai: "Not much food, many restrictions.

"Here even a proud man bows his head low."

Tour Guide: Thanks, Lui and Hai, for your help with translating today. How do reading these walls make you feel?

Student: It makes me mad. Why did Americans do this to the Chinese?

Tour Guide: One thing we can learn from history is mistakes we have made. That's why your teacher brought you here to the Angel Island Immigration Center. And that's why the words that are carved into this wall are preserved, so we can remember our past and learn from it.

Student: Thanks for showing us around. I will never forget it.

©RBP Books   www.summerbridgeactivities.com   Reading Connection—Grade 5—RBP0202

Uncovering Ideas

1. Why do you think the Chinese people wrote on the walls of the barracks?

   _____

   _____

   _____

2. What does "I feel like a fish out of water" mean?

   _____

   _____

   _____

3. Name three things that writers of these poems worried about.

   _____

   _____

   _____

Connecting to Life

1. Imagine you could talk to the Chinese people who wrote these poems. What would you ask them?

   _____

   _____

   _____

2. Can you think of another group of people that had an experience like this? Who were they, and what happened?

   _____

   _____

   _____

Reading Skills Builder

WANT AD

Dog Walker—Too busy to walk your dog? I can help! 2 years experience teaching dog obedience classes. Good with large and small dogs. Affordable—$10 an hour for each dog. Call Kyle Jones. Day: 466-4883 Eve: 473-3221

This ad needs to be shorter. Rewrite it to make it only three lines. Use abbreviations if you want.

_____

_____

_____

Word Work

Put these words from the story into the sentences. Use each word only once.

ambition	humility	restriction	unbearable
scarcity	pierced	detained	ideal

1. The man was _____ from getting home because traffic was slow.

2. Anne's head was pounding; the pain was _____.

3. The family looked at many houses until they found the _____ one.

4. Erin thought the No Trespassing sign was an unfair _____.

5. During the Great Depression, there was a _____ of food and money.

6. The dancer's greatest _____ was to become a famous ballerina.

7. It's better to talk about yourself with _____ than to brag.

From Tomboy to Ballerina

By Alisha Golden

Is there something you can't imagine yourself becoming?

When I was young, I never wanted to be a dancer. I was more of a tomboy, always wanting to do whatever sports my brother did, like skateboarding, rollerblading, and soccer. In my mind, ballet or dance was for girls. I'm a girl, but I didn't see myself as one of "them": a girly, giggly, cootie-hater. I was one of the guys and proud of it. Dance was for sissies.

I tried all sports and did OK, but I was never very good at any of them except soccer. There was always just one problem: I'm very small. I was tough, but I didn't have the mass to back it up. I had spunk but no muscle. So, when my long soccer career ended, I was crushed. There was nothing really left for me to do but dance. People had told me my whole life that my body was built for dance. My long skinny legs, firm slender arms, and graceful neck seemed made for ballet. Without soccer to play anymore, it seemed that fate was against me. By this time, I was 11 years old and starting to appreciate being a girl more, so I gave in to my mom's wish and decided to try dancing.

In the beginning, I was clumsy and had absolutely no sense of balance. I didn't have a graceful bone in my body. All I knew how to do was run and kick, and there was none of that in ballet. My first few months of weekly lessons were a disaster, but I never quit. If you could choose one word to describe my attitude, it would be stubborn. I was never going to quit even if it killed me. Because of my dedication, hard work, and resolve, I got better and better, until I found myself in a dance studio almost daily, doing nothing but dancing.

I love to dance. Sometimes it is just plain hard, and other days, I really enjoy myself. Our teacher yells out corrections and choreographed steps to us as we dance. The violinist plays beautifully on his instrument. The notes carry me into the sky. I feel as if I am flying on the music. The faint smell of sweat permeates the air around me and fills my nose. It has a sort of sweetness. Breathing heavily and sweating, I feel more alive than ever. Fatigue is miles away. I am going to be a ballerina. I can never give up this passion, even though the pain in my toes stings and screams for me to stop. Soaring, I cannot feel the ground beneath me. My tutu rustles softly as my toe shoes patter on the floor with every step. My legs and arms move and extend in harmony with the music. Every part of my body moves as gracefully as a June breeze. I love to dance!

Uncovering Ideas

1. Why didn't the author want to be a balle-rina at first?

   _____

2. Which statement best tells why the author became a good dancer?
   a. She had the best teacher in the state.
   b. She had dedication, hard work, and desire.
   c. She was forced to dance.
   d. She wanted to impress a cute boy with her excellent dancing skills.

3. Find a sentence in the story that shows how the author feels about dancing now.

   _____

Connecting to Life

1. What does this story remind you of?

   _____

2. On another sheet of paper, write about a time you or someone you know learned to do something new. What was it like?

Reading Skills Builder

Authors use **sensory words** to help you see what they see. Sensory words describe what the author sees, hears, smells, tastes, or touches. Under each category, write the words from the last paragraph of the story that belong under each of the senses.

see _____

hear _____

smell _____

touch _____

Think of an activity, sport, or fun thing that you've done recently. Fill in details about what you saw, heard, smelled, felt, or tasted.

see _____

hear _____

smell _____

touch _____

taste _____

Adding sensory details to writing helps the reader to visualize what you are writing. Now write one paragraph adding all these details together.

_____

_____

_____

Word Work

Add the suffix **-ful** to these words:

1. wonder _____
2. power _____
3. help _____
4. hand _____
5. mouth _____
6. grace _____
7. dread _____
8. care _____

Use words from above in these sentences.

1. Juan wasn't _____ as he picked the rose, and he pricked his finger.
2. Tyler picked a _____ of daisies and gave them to his mother.
3. The ballerina's dance was _____.
4. Janie did the dishes because she wanted to be _____ to her mother.
5. Sara handed me the ice cream, and I took a huge _____.

The Red Thread of Courage

Adapted from Sara Cone Bryant, *How to Tell Stories to Children, and Some Stories to Tell*

Is it possible for soldiers to respect the people they are fighting against?

Years ago, English troops in India were fighting against some of the native tribes. One tribe in particular proved to be strong enemies. They were good fighters and clever at setting up ambushes. The tribe was made up of people from the hill-country, and the English called them Hillsmen. The English knew very little about them, except their courage, but they had noticed one peculiar custom. After some battles, the Hillsmen marked the bodies of their greatest chiefs killed in battle by tying a red thread about the wrist. This was the highest tribute the Hillsmen could pay a hero.

One day, a small band of English soldiers had marched a long way into the hill country after the enemy. By afternoon they found themselves in a part of the country strange even to the guides. The men moved slowly and cautiously forward, fearing an ambush. The trail led into a narrow valley with steep, rocky sides topped with woods where the enemy might easily hide.

The soldiers were ordered to advance more quickly to get out of the dangerous place. They marched until they found the passage divided in two by a big three-cornered boulder that seemed to rise from the midst of the valley. The main line of men kept to the right. To keep from crowding the path, a sergeant and 11 men took the left. They would go around the rock and meet the rest of the group beyond it.

They had been in the path only a few minutes when they saw that the rock was not a single boulder at all. It was an arm of the left wall of the valley, and they were marching into a deep ravine with no outlet except the way they had come in. Both sides were sheer rock, with thick trees at the top; in front of them the ground rose in a steep hill, bare of woods. As they looked up, they saw that the top of the hill was barricaded by the trunks of trees and guarded by a strong body of Hillsmen. As the English hesitated, a shower of spears fell from the woods' edge. The place was a death trap.

The officer in command of the main body saw the danger and signaled to the sergeant to retreat. But the signal was misunderstood! The men took it for the signal to charge. Without a moment's pause, they charged straight up the slope, cheering as they ran.

Some were killed by spears that were thrown from the cliffs before they had gone halfway. Some were stabbed as they reached the crest and hurled backward from the precipice. Two or three got to the top and fought hand to hand with the Hillsmen. They were outnumbered seven to one, but when the last of the English soldiers lay dead, twice their number of Hillsmen lay dead around them!

When the relief party reached the spot later that day, they found the bodies of their comrades. They were full of wounds. Some were draped over and in the barricade, and others fallen on the rocks below. But around the wrist of each man was tied a red thread.

Uncovering Ideas

1. Who is this battle between, and where is each side from?

   _____

   _____

   _____

2. Why do you think the Hillsmen won this battle?

   _____

   _____

   _____

3. What does the title "The Red Thread of Courage" have to do with the story?

   _____

   _____

   _____

Connecting to Life

1. Compare this story of battle with another that you have read about or seen in a movie. How are they the same, and how are they different? Use the Venn Diagram below to help you.

   _____

   _____

   _____

Battle between
English and Hillsmen

Another battle
I've read about or seen

Reading Skills Builder

An **entry word** is a word you look up in the dictionary. It is the simplest form of the word. If you want to find out what *costly* means, you would look up the word *cost* in the dictionary.

What would the entry word be for each of these words?

1. celebrated ___**celebrate**___
2. happier _____
3. chilly _____
4. classical _____
5. faster_____
6. couples_____
7. deformed_____

Word Work

Find these words in the story and see if you can decide what they mean. If you need to, use a dictionary. Then use each word in one of the sentences below.

precipice

barricade

ravine

1. He tried to stop the enemy by putting up a _____ to keep him out.

2. The rock rolled all the way to the bottom of a deep _____.

3. While standing on the _____ of the hill, the boy could see all the way to the next town.

Now use one of the words to write a sentence of your own.

_____

_____

_____

Yuri's Night: Celebrating Space Travel

By Joseph Soderborg

What do you think it would it be like to orbit the earth?

> *A day will come when beings … shall stand upon this earth as one stands upon a footstool, and shall laugh and reach out their hands amid the stars.*
> H. G. Wells, *The Discovery of the Future*, 1901

H. G. Wells said these words 60 years before Yuri Gagarin orbited the earth. Yuri was the first man in space. As he circled the planet, his comrades below asked what he could see. "I see the earth," he said. "It's so beautiful."

Yuri Gagarin was born in a small home on a Russian farm. He became one of the Soviet Union's heroes after his space travel. After he returned from space, he traveled the globe, speaking out for world peace and the beauty of the earth. Now he is honored each April 12 in a celebration called Yuri's Night.

Many countries celebrate Yuri's Night. There are parties at dance clubs, universities like North Carolina State, and even in the city center of Stockholm, Sweden. Centers of the space industry celebrate. The Mission Control Center in Houston, Texas; the Space Dynamics Laboratory at Logan, Utah; and the Russian Cosmonaut Training Center throw parties. So do people in Manzini, Swaziland; Neuquen, Argentina; and Izmar, Turkey.

In 2003, 51 parties were held in 23 countries. Party-goers joined in both fun and serious ceremonies. The party in Portland, Oregon, showed off Bob McGown's famous meteorite collection. In Uzbekistan people gathered for a huge banquet. They gave speeches and toasted space exploration. Some Yuri's Night parties had children's activities like looking through telescopes and games. In San Francisco, people celebrated with a costume contest and dancing. Yuri's Night in Tokyo had free food and a quiz tournament about space. Yuri's Night 2003 was dedicated to the crew of the space shuttle *Columbia*.

Yuri's Night actually celebrates two historic events: Yuri Gagarin's orbit around the earth and the launch of the first space shuttle. Both events took place on April 12, exactly 20 years apart. The first shuttle to fly was the *Columbia*.

The *Columbia* disaster reminds us how dangerous space exploration is. Yuri's Night lets people celebrate brave heroes who risk their lives to explore the unknown. Although Yuri Gagarin flew into space and returned safely, he was killed in 1968 while test-piloting a new jet.

You can plan your own Yuri's Night party. Use your imagination and have fun. There's also a website where you can contact other people and organize your celebration. It's at *www.yurisnight.net*.

www.summerbridgeactivities.com   **Reading Connection—Grade 5—RBP0202**

Uncovering Ideas

1. Where was Yuri Gagarin born?

   _____

   _____

2. Name two places where Yuri's Night has been celebrated.

   _____

   _____

3. According to the story, why might Yuri's Night celebrations have been more serious in 2003?

   _____

   _____

   _____

Connecting to Life

1. Imagine you have the chance to orbit the earth in the space shuttle. How do you think you would feel? Describe what you think the earth looks like from up in space.

   _____

   _____

   _____

2. What does this story remind you of?

   _____

   _____

Reading Skills Builder

In the News

A. Forty-Year-Old Cat Outlives Owner

B. Man Claims Elvis Works at Local McDonald's

C. Santa Claus Protests War at the North Pole

D. Utah Jazz Take the Court by Storm in Play-off Game

E. Mayor Caught Running Red Light

F. Weather Watch: Flash Flood Alert for Residents of Aqua County

---

1. In which article would you find out what the mayor's been up to lately? _____

2. In which article would you expect to find tips about how to avoid natural disasters?

   _____

3. Which article contains sports information?

   _____

4. Which story do you think is the least important?

   _____

5. Which article is the most important?

   _____

Word Work

The word part **ast-** means "star."

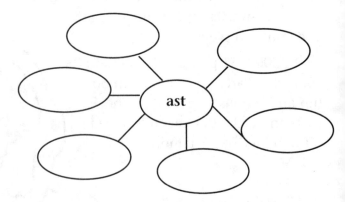

1. Find other words that have the word part **ast-** in them. See how many have something to do with stars or space.

The Burning of the Rice Fields

Adapted from Sara Cone Bryant, *How to Tell Stories to Children, and Some Stories to Tell*

How can something good come from something bad?

Once there was an old man who lived up on a mountain, far away in Japan. All around his little house the mountain was flat. The ground there was rich, and it was here that the people who lived in the village at the mountain's foot planted their rice fields. Mornings and evenings, the old man and his little grandson used to look far down on the people at work in the village. From here the could also watch the blue sea which lay all round the land, so close that there was no room for fields at the mountain's foot.

The little boy loved the rice fields. He knew that food for all the people came from the fields, and he often helped his grandfather watch over them.

One day, the grandfather was standing alone, looking far down at the people and out at the sea. Suddenly, he saw something very strange, far off where the sea and sky meet. Something like a great cloud was rising there, as if the sea were lifting itself into the sky. The old man put his hands to his eyes and looked again, hard as his old sight could. Then he turned and ran to the house. "Yone, Yone!" he cried to his grandson, "bring a brand from the hearth!"

The little grandson could not imagine what his grandfather wanted with fire, but he ran quickly and brought the smoldering brand. The old man already had one and was running for the rice fields. Yone ran after him. To his horror, he saw his grandfather thrust his burning brand into the ripe, dry rice where it stood.

"Grandfather, Grandfather!" screamed the little boy, "What are you doing?"

"Quick, set fire! Thrust your brand in!" said the grandfather.

Yone thought his dear grandfather had lost his mind, and he began to sob. But he always obeyed, so through his tears, he thrust his torch in. The sharp flames ran up the dry stalks, red and yellow. In an instant, the field was ablaze, and thick black smoke began to pour up from the mountainside. It rose like a cloud, black and fierce, and in no time the people below saw that their precious rice fields were on fire. Ah, how they ran! Men, women, and children climbed the mountain, running as fast as they could to save the rice. Not one soul stayed behind.

When they came to the mountaintop and saw the beautiful rice crop in flame, they cried, "Who has done this? How did it happen?"

"I set the fire," said the old man, very solemnly. The little grandson sobbed beside him, "Grandfather set the fire."

When the people gathered fiercely around the old man and cried, "Why? Why?" he only turned and pointed to the sea. "Look!" he said.

They all turned and looked. There, where the blue sea had lain so calm, a mighty wall of water, reaching from earth to sky, was rolling in. No one could scream, so terrible was the sight. The wall of water rolled in on the land, passed over the place where the village had been, and broke with an awful sound on the mountainside. One more wave came, and one more. Then all was water, as far as they could see below. The village where they had been was under the sea.

But the people were all safe. And when they saw what the old man had done, they honored him above all men for the quick wit which had saved them all from the tidal wave.

© RBP Books   www.summerbridgeactivities.com   Reading Connection—Grade 5—RBP0202

Uncovering Ideas

1. Why were the rice fields important to the people?

   _____

   _____

2. Why did the old man and his grandson burn the rice fields?

   _____

3. What do you think would have happened if the old man hadn't set the field on fire?

   _____

   _____

Connecting to Life

1. In this story, something bad happens that turns out to be a good thing. What is another story or movie you've seen that ended in a way you didn't expect?

   _____

   _____

Reading Skills Builder

A. June 30, 2003

B. Accommodation Airlines
3000 Airport Drive
Flounder, Florida 83909

C. Dear Sir,

D. I am writing to complain about how I was treated on my flight from Memphis, Tennessee, to Pocatello, Idaho. The flight attendants refused to let me carry my precious poodle Bisquit on the plane. Bisquit is very well-behaved and doesn't bark unless spooked. Because she fit easily in my carry-on bag, I didn't think twice about bringing her on the plane. But the attendant said Bisquit wasn't a carry-on because she is a living thing. Why should it matter whether my "carry-on" is living or not? What if I had taken my plant on the plane inside my bag? Because of your rule, Bisquit had to stay behind on the trip, which caused her and me great pain. I hope you will consider allowing small dogs on the plane as carry-ons—or else change the name of your airline.

E. In earnest,

F. Mrs. Carrie A. Poodle

1. Where is the date located in the letter?

   _____

2. Where is the body, or main part, of the letter? _____

3. What is the mood of the writer of this letter?

   _____

4. Where did Mrs. Poodle travel?

   _____

Word Work

Find a word that has the same connection as the underlined pair before it:

1. A <u>rice field</u> in <u>Japan</u> is like a
   _____**potato field**_____ in Idaho.

2. A <u>car</u> to a <u>mechanic</u> is like a
   _____ to a surgeon.

3. A <u>parachute</u> to a <u>skydiver</u> is like a
   _____ to a deep sea diver.

4. <u>Socks</u> are to <u>feet</u> like _____ are to hands.

5. <u>Air</u> is to a <u>bird</u> what _____ is to a fish.

Annabel Lee

By Edgar Allan Poe

This is an example of a poem that has rhythm. Poets think about the sounds of words and how to put them together so their poem sounds musical. Read this poem out loud. Try beating the words out like a drum, or reading the poem like you are singing a rap song. Each syllable should be a beat. What kind of rhythm does it make?

It was many and many a year ago,
In a kingdom by the sea,
That a maiden there lived whom you may know
By the name of Annabel Lee;
And this maiden she lived with no other thought
Than to love and be loved by me.

I was a child and she was a child,
In this kingdom by the sea,
But we loved with a love that was more than love,
I and my Annabel Lee;
With a love that the winged seraphs of heaven
Coveted her and me.

And this was the reason that, long ago,
In this kingdom by the sea,
A wind blew out of a cloud, chilling
My beautiful Annabel Lee;
So that her highborn kinsman came
And bore her away from me,
To shut her up in a sepulchre
In this kingdom by the sea.

The angels, not half so happy in heaven,
Went envying her and me;
Yes! that was the reason (as all men know,
In this kingdom by the sea)
That the wind came out of the cloud by night,
Chilling and killing my Annabel Lee.

But our love it was stronger by far than the love
Of those who were older than we,
Of many far wiser than we;
And neither the angels in heaven above,
Nor the demons down under the sea,
Can ever dissever my soul from the soul
Of the beautiful Annabel Lee:

For the moon never beams without bringing me dreams
Of the beautiful Annabel Lee;
And the stars never rise, but I feel the bright eyes
Of the beautiful Annabel Lee;
And so, all the night-tide, I lie down by the side
Of my darling—my darling—my life and my bride,
In the sepulchre there by the sea,
In her tomb by the sounding sea.

Uncovering Ideas

1. Choose the best statement that tells how the poet feels about Annabel Lee

   _____ **a.** Their love changed like the ocean.

   _____ **b.** He was forgetting about her.

   _____ **c.** Their love was so strong that even the angels couldn't break it.

   _____ **d.** He loves her like a sister.

2. What do you think happened to Annabel Lee?

   _____

   _____

3. The poet creates a **mood** with this poem. What kind of mood does he create? Write three words that help create this mood.

   _____

   _____

Connecting to Life

1. Edgar Allan Poe talks about how he dreams of Annabel Lee. In the space below, draw a picture of either his dream or a dream you have had. Explain the dream in a complete sentence under your drawing.

   ┌─────────────────────────────────────┐
   │   │
   │   │
   │   │
   │   │
   │   │
   │   │
   │   │
   │   │
   │   │
   └─────────────────────────────────────┘

   _____

Reading Skills Builder

Put each line of the address in the right order.

_____ Soldiers Fort, Nevada

_____ Emily Anderson

_____ 98883

_____ Advertising Director

_____ Plastic Grapes Inc.

_____ P.O. Box 202

Word Work

A. How many syllables are in each line? Count by reading out loud.

__11__ It was many and many a year ago

_____ In a kingdom by the sea,

_____ That a maiden there lived whom you may know

_____ By the name of Annabel Lee;

B. Do you see a pattern?

C. Syllable Sounds

Separate the parts of the word by where syllables are.

How many syllables are in each word?

Word	Break apart by syllables	Number of syllables
kingdom	**king / dom**	2
bringing		
many		
maiden		
Annabel		
dreams		
dissever		

Why the Night-hawk's Wings Are Beautiful

Frank B. Linderman, from *Indian Why Stories*

What would it be like to travel with a Native American village?

I WAS awakened by the voice of the camp-crier, and although it was yet dark I listened to his message.

The camp was to move. All were to go to the mouth of the Maria's—"The River That Scolds at the Other"...

On through the camp the crier rode, and behind him the lodge-fires glowed in answer to his call. The village was awake, and soon the thunder of hundreds of hooves told me that the pony-bands were being driven into camp, where the faithful were being roped for the journey. Fires flickered in the now fading darkness, and down came the lodges as though wizard hands had touched them. Before the sun had come to light the world, we were on our way to "The River That Scolds at the Other."

Not a cloud was in the sky, and the wind was still. The sun came and touched the plains and hilltops with the light that makes all wild things glad. Here and there a jackrabbit scurried away, often followed by a pack of dogs, and sometimes, though not often, they were overtaken and devoured on the spot. Bands of graceful antelope bounded out of our way, stopping on a knoll to watch the strange procession with won-dering eyes, and once we saw a dust-cloud raised by a moving herd of buffalo in the distance.

So the day wore on, the scene constantly changing as we traveled. Wolves and coyotes looked at us from almost every knoll and hilltop; and sage-hens sneaked to cover among the patches of sage-brush, scarcely ten feet away from our ponies. Toward sundown we reached a grove of cottonwoods near the mouth of the Maria's, and in an incredibly short space of time the lodges took form. Soon, from out the tops of a hundred camps, smoke was curling just as though the lodges had been there always, and would forever remain.

As soon as supper was over I found the children, and together we sought War Eagle's lodge. He was in a happy mood and insisted upon smoking two pipes before commencing his story-telling. At last he said:

"To-night I shall tell you why the Night-hawk wears fine clothes. My grandfather told me about it when I was young. I am sure you have seen the Night-hawk sailing over you, dipping and making that strange noise. Of course there is a reason for it."

(to be continued)

Uncovering Ideas

1. Write a summary of what happens in this story.

   _____

   _____

   _____

2. The people in this story are traveling. Pretend you are in this group, and you need to draw a map of your journey to help other people find where to go. Use natural landmarks, trees, animals, and names of things from the story itself.

   [ ]

3. The storyteller is about to tell how the hawk got its fine clothes. What do you think the reason is?

   _____

   _____

Connecting to Life

1. The travelers meet different animals along their way. Write about an animal you have seen in the wild, or in a zoo. Tell what you like about this animal.

   _____

   _____

   _____

   _____

Reading Skills Builder

Put the following words in alphabetical order

1.

   ____ fit

   ____ flake

   ____ flank

   ____ flash

   ____ flapper

Word Work

Circle the best definition for each of the words from the story below.

1. procession
   a march   a meeting   a disease

2. knoll
   river   small animal   hill

3. devour
   to fill   to eat up   to watch

4. commence
   to end   to shake   to begin

5. scene
   a cup   to keep in order   setting

Frank B.Linderman, from *Indian Why Stories*

"Old-man was traveling one day in the springtime; but the weather was fine for that time of year. He stopped often and spoke to the bird-people and to the animal-people, for he was in good humor that day. He talked pleasantly with the trees, and his heart grew tender. That is, he had good thoughts; and of course they made him happy. Finally he felt tired and sat down to rest on a big, round stone—the kind of stone our white friend there calls a boulder. Here he rested for a while, but the stone was cold, and he felt it through his robe; so he said:

"'Stone, you seem cold today. You may have my robe. I have hundreds of robes in my camp, and I don't need this one at all.' That was a lie he told about having so many robes. All he had was the one he wore.

"He spread his robe over the stone, and then started down the hill, naked, for it was really a fine day. But storms hide in the mountains, and are never far away when it is springtime. Soon it began to snow—then the wind blew from the north with a good strength behind it. Old-man said:

"'Well, I guess I do need that robe myself, after all. That stone never did anything for me anyhow. Nobody is ever good to a stone. I'll just go back and get my robe.'

"Back he went and found the stone. Then he pulled the robe away, and wrapped it about himself. Ho! But that made the stone angry— Ho! Old-man started to run down the hill, and the stone ran after him. Ho! It was a funny race they made, over the grass, over smaller stones, and over logs that lay in the way, but Old-man managed to keep ahead until he stubbed his toe on a big sage-brush and fell—'swow!'

"'Now I have you!' cried the stone— 'now I'll kill you, too! Now I will teach you to give presents and then take them away,' and the stone rolled right on top of Old-man, and sat on his back.

"It was a big stone, you see, and Old-man couldn't move it at all. He tried to throw off the stone but failed. He squirmed and twisted—no use—the stone held him fast. He called the stone some names that are good; but that never helps any. At last he began to call:

"'Help! Help! Help!' but nobody heard him except the Night-hawk, and he told the Old-man that he would help him all he could; so he flew away up in the air—so far that he looked like a black speck. Then he came down straight and struck that rock an awful blow—'swow!'—and broke it in two pieces. Indeed he did. The blow was so great that it spoiled the Night-hawk's bill, forever—made it queer in shape, and jammed his head, so that it is queer, too. But he broke the rock, and Old-man stood upon his feet.

"'Thank you, Brother Night-hawk, ' said Old-man, 'now I will do something for you. I am going to make you different from other birds— make you so people will always notice you.'

"You know that when you break a rock the powdered stone is white, like snow; and there is always some of the white powder whenever you break a rock, by pounding it. Well, Old-man took some of the fine powdered stone and shook it on the Night-hawk's wings in spots and stripes— made the great white stripes you have seen on his wings, and told him that no other bird could have such marks on his clothes.

"All the Night-hawk's children dress the same way now; and they always will as long as there are Night-hawks. Of course their clothes make them proud; and that is why they keep at flying over people's heads—soaring and dipping and turning all the time, to show off their pretty wings."

37

Uncovering Ideas

1. This story is an example of a myth. A myth is a story people tell to explain why something is the way it is. On another sheet of paper, make up your own story to explain something. Here are a few examples: How did the skunk get its stripe? How did the giraffe get its long neck?

2. At what time of year did this story take place?

_____

3. According to this story, why are the nighthawk's wings beautiful? Circle the right answer.

   a. he had a good-looking hawk dad

   b. to attract female birds

   c. because the Old-Man sprinkled stone powder on them

   d. it catches snow on its wings

4. Why did the old man give the stone his robe?

_____

Connecting to Life

1. People in many cultures tell stories as a way of passing down history or teaching something. Does your cultural or ethnic group tell stories? Do you have family stories that are passed down? On a separate piece of paper, write an example of a story that was told to you. Why was the story told? Where were you when you heard it?

2. For what purposes did the native people tell this story?

_____

3. What would you do if a huge rock was chasing you down a mountain?

_____

Reading Skills Builder

Put the following in order, starting with which happened first.

_____ The stone rolled on the old man's back.

_____ The old man sprinkled rock powder on the hawk's wings.

_____ The old man took his robe back from the stone.

_____ The hawk broke the stone in two.

_____ The old man gave his robe to the stone.

_____ The old man stubbed his toe on a big sagebrush.

Word Work

Change the boldface word into an adverb by adding an -ly.

1. The sun is **bright**.
   The sun shines _____.

2. The girl was **happy**.
   The girl sang _____.

3. We were **careful**.
   He washed the china _____.

4. The service was **quick**.
   The kids ran _____ to the candy.

5. The food tasted **awful**.
   The music sounds _____ loud.

6. The cookies were **sweet**.
   The girl sang _____.

7. The band was **loud**.
   The man sang the song _____.

8. The dog was **wild**.
   The dog ran _____ in the yard.

9. The child was **quiet**.
   Do your homework _____.

10. She looked **wonderful**.
    He played the piano_____.

An Empire of Chocolate

By Alisha Golden

Do you know where the Hershey bar came from?

When you think of Hershey Chocolate, what's the first thing that comes to mind? I bet you don't think of Milton Snavely Hershey. He was the man who started his own chocolate business a long time ago.

Milton grew up on a farm in the small town of Hockersville, Pennsylvania. Like many farm boys, he learned about hard work and chores at a young age. These taught him valuable lessons that would help him in life.

He went to school until he was in fourth grade. Then his father put him to work as a printer's apprentice. When it became clear that his future was not in printing, Milton became an apprentice to a candy maker.

He found that his talent lay in creating and selling delicious candies. At age 18, he opened his own candy shop in Philadelphia, Pennsylvania. When the business failed after six years, he moved to Denver, Colorado. There, he learned how to make caramels. He moved on to Chicago, New Orleans, and New York City, trying to establish a candy business in each city. When these all failed, he decided to return to his roots. He moved to Lancaster, Pennsylvania, in 1886 and raised enough money to make caramels. He named his business the Lancaster Caramel Company and became a first-class candy maker.

Milton got the idea of making chocolate at the Chicago International Exposition in 1893. While there, he saw a German chocolate making machine on exhibit. He bought the equipment and soon began producing chocolate coatings for his caramels. In 1894, the Hershey Chocolate Company was born.

During this time, he also married Catherine (Kitty) Sweeney in New York City. Milton was 41 years old.

In 1900, Milton sold his caramel company. He used the one million dollars he made to start his chocolate empire in his hometown, Derry Church. It was a great spot to start his business because the fresh milk produced by local farmers helped create superior chocolates.

The chocolate business continued to grow, as did the town surrounding it. A department store, a school, churches, a park, a bank, a zoo, and a trolley system were all built within a short time with Milton's money and direction. When the town needed to be renamed, his employees decided to name it Hershey, in honor of the man who had started it all.

Milton Hershey was never able to have any of his own children, so he decided to establish a school for homeless boys. On November 15, 1909, the Milton Hershey School opened. Milton wanted his "boys" to learn a good work ethic as he had, so when not studying or doing their lessons, the boys were given farm chores.

Milton Hershey never wanted to be famous, but he was willing to work hard. Because of that he earned great fortune, which he used to benefit those around him. He died a prosperous man on October 13, 1945, at the age of 88.

Uncovering Ideas

1. Make a timeline of the important events in the life of Milton Hershey.

Born 1857

2. When did Milton decide to start making chocolates and not just caramels?

   _____

   _____

3. What are some reasons you think Milton was successful in his business?

   _____

   _____

Connecting to Life

1. Imagine you invented a new kind of candy. What would it be, and what would it taste like or do? Draw a picture of the candy you will invent. Include its name, and explain why it is special.

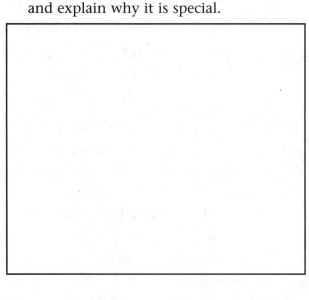

   _____

   _____

Reading Skills Builder

Sound out the license plates to figure out what they mean.

1. ABNRML _____

2. ENJYNLF _____

3. EZ2PLEZ _____

4. HOLIKOW _____

5. IMZ14U _____

6. IXLR8 _____

Word Work

Spelling Rule: Drop the **y**, add an **i**, then add a different ending.

1. accompany + ed

   accompanied

2. worry + ed

   _____

3. city + s

   _____

4. bury + ed

   _____

5. luxury + ous

   _____

6. emergency + es

   _____

Reading Connection—Grade 5—RBP0202   www.summerbridgeactivities.com   ©RBP Books

Kids Say Good-bye to Loveable Livestock

By Jenie Skoy, as staff writer for *The Preston Citizen*

What if you had to say good-bye to your favorite pet?

Dusty kids in Wranglers and cowboy boots, with sunburned faces and wind-blown hair, said their last good-byes to their cows, pigs, and lambs at the Preston County Fair on Friday night.

But eleven-year-old Adam Swann wasn't ready to say good-bye to his friendly bucket cow, Big Red. Adam was planning on sleeping overnight at the fairgrounds with his cow before they took him away, but the man who bought Big Red had to leave town, so he took the cow earlier than planned.

"Adam asked where his cow was," Adam's dad, Lyle, said. "So I told him, and he was just brokenhearted. He didn't get to sleep until 11 p.m., and it was out of exhaustion."

Adam said it was hard to let Big Red go because he had become a friend.

"He'd put his nose up to me. He didn't care if I put my arms around his neck and hugged him or kinda leaned against him if I was tired," said Adam.

"Everywhere he went, the cow went with him," said Lyle.

Christie Owen, who won Reserve Champion with her steer Dusty, said she'd been working with her cow all summer. Owen spent time Thursday hair-spraying and combing her cow's hair for the upcoming auction, where Dusty would be showcased as one of the finest to bid on.

"His hair won't go right," said Owen, brushing the bovine's hair between its ears into a kind of mohawk. Not only was Dusty's hair stubborn, but he was stubborn, too.

"He was either kicking me or licking me," said Owen.

Buckey J. McKay, 14, had raised his steer Wild Thing since its mother was killed when the calf was two weeks old.

"He's the tamest pet," said McKay. "He will follow you around and eat right out of your hand." Wild Thing ate anything he could find, including paper and plastic, and sometimes the cow was cannibalistic, eating hamburgers that McKay fed him.

"I wasn't too sad to give him up," said McKay."What are you going to do with a 1200 lb. steer hanging around?" McKay took second place in showmanship with Wild Thing.

Shauna Jepsen, 11, changed her 250 lb. pink pig's name from Wilber to Mike Tyson the day she took him to the fair and put him in a pen with the other pigs.

"He got into fights with every pig he could find," said Jepsen. The pig had a split personality: softhearted Wilber at home, but a fighter in public. "They think he is just trying to protect me," she explained. "He is gentle at the house. You could rub his belly, and he would roll over like a dog."

The pig was auctioned off Friday night, and Shauna had to say good-bye to her friend. Now, when she gets homesick for Wilber she pulls out some pictures of him so she is not so sad.

Stuart Parkinson, extension agent for Franklin County and who has seen some of the children say good-bye, explains it this way: "Letting go teaches kids a valuable lesson. It's when they have to walk away (from their animals) that they learn about life, about attachment and how to deal with sadness."

Uncovering Ideas

1. Which statement best tells what this story is about?

_____ how to train cows and pigs for the fair

_____ how much to pay at an animal auction

_____ why people and animals don't get along

_____ how even farm animals can become pets

2. Why are the kids in this story sad?

_____

_____

_____

3. Match the name of the animal with its owner

Wild Thing	Christie Owen
Big Red	Buckey J. McKay
Wilber	Adam Swann
Dusty	Shauna Jepsen

4. What do you think Stuart Parkinson means when he said: "Letting go teaches kids a valuable lesson"?

_____

_____

_____

Connecting to Life

1. Have you ever owned a pet? Who was your first pet, and what was his/her name? If you haven't had a pet, write about the pet of a friend or neighbor.

_____

_____

_____

Word Work

Use your dictionary to help find the best definition for these words:

1. bowlegged

_____

2. bull

_____

3. Jersey

_____

4. lasso

_____

5. bridle

_____

Reading Skills Builder

Below are some examples of slang words that cowboys might use. Match the word on the right with the definition to the left. Check your own work when you finish.

1. ____ bronc
2. ____ chuck
3. ____ dogie
4. ____ mustang
5. ____ on the dodge
6. ____ outlaw
7. ____ quirt
8. ____ road agent
9. ____ shindig
10. ____ tenderfoot
11. ____ the whole kit and caboodle
12. ____ cowjuice

A. a cowboy dance
B. food
C. the entire thing
D. milk
E. a calf whose mother has left it
F. a wild animal or criminal
G. a cowboy's whip
H. a wild horse
I. hiding from the police
J. a person who is new to a job
K. a wild horse
L. a robber

Amelia Earhart: A Pioneer in Flight

By Alisha Golden

An aviator *is a person who flies a plane. Amelia Earhart became one of the most famous women aviators in the world by just doing what she loved best. What do you enjoy doing? Do you think you can someday make a career out of what you love, just like Amelia Earhart did?*

Amelia Earhart saw her first plane at a state fair when she was ten years old.

"It was a thing of rusty wire and wood and looked not at all interesting," she said about it. It wasn't until a decade later, while attending a stunt-flying exhibition, that she really became interested in flying.

She rode in an airplane for the first time in 1920. After that, she was hooked. As a social worker, Amelia had never had any experience with airplanes. Determined to learn, she took her first lesson on January 3, 1921. In just six months, she saved enough money to buy her very own plane. It was a bright yellow Kinner Airster nicknamed "Canary." She set her first women's record in it by flying to an altitude of 14,000 feet.

Amelia flew constantly. Her hard work paid off in April 1928 when a book publisher and publicist named George P. Putnam asked if she would fly across the Atlantic. Her answer was "Yes!" She was only a passenger on the historical flight between Newfoundland and Wales, but she returned to the United States a celebrity.

From that point on, Earhart's life centered on flying. She became popular as she won competitions and awards. Though she had been a shy tomboy, people thought she was witty, charming, and intelligent. Her fans loved the fact that she looked so much like Charles Lindbergh, another great aviator

of the time. Many people called her "Lady Lindy."

Amelia and George Putnam married on February 7, 1931. Then, together they planned her solo trek across the icy Atlantic, which began on May 20, 1932. When she returned home, the media surrounded her as President Herbert Hoover awarded her a gold medal from the National Geographic Society. More medals followed. But she didn't stop there. On January 11, 1935, she became the first person to fly solo from Honolulu, Hawaii, to Oakland, California.

As Amelia drew close to her 40th birthday, she set a new goal. She wanted to be the first woman to fly around the world. Despite a failed first attempt in March 1937, and a damaged plane, a stubborn and determined Earhart departed from Miami, Florida, on June 1. With her was her navigator, Fred Noonan. They had completed all but 7,000 miles of the 29,000 mile journey when they disappeared over the Pacific Ocean. Heading for a small island, she missed it because of cloudy conditions and never landed. A rescue attempt began immediately. It soon became the most extensive search for a single plane ever made by the U.S. Navy. They never found Amelia Earhart or her plane, but she lives on as a legend in aviation history.

Uncovering Ideas

1. Make a timeline of the events that led Amelia Earhart to become an aviator.

2. What did Amelia Earhart do before she became an aviator?

   _____

3. According to the story, how did the public see Amelia Earhart?

   _____

   _____

Connecting to Life

1. People have searched for many years to discover Amelia Earhart's plane, but no one has found it yet. There are many theories about what happened to Amelia Earhart. Make up your own theory of what you think happened.

   _____

   _____

   _____

   _____

2. On a separate sheet of paper, write a newspaper article reporting Amelia Earhart's disappearance over the ocean. Use the five W's in your story: who, what, when, why, and where.

   Earhart Disappears over the Pacific

   Story by: (your name)_____

   Story: (two paragraphs)

Reading Skills Builder

Following Directions:
Join us all at the Darvis Family Reunion. Here are the directions to Uncle Brigham's house:

   Follow I-30 until the Ugly Mile Exit.
   Turn right onto Ugly Mile Road.
   Go 7 miles south until you reach a traffic light.
   At the traffic light, turn right onto Kickin' Chicken Drive.
   Go until you reach the Fruit Loop subdivision and turn left.
   Take your first right at Papaya Street. Our house is the fifth on the right.

1. How far do you travel on Ugly Mile Road?

   _____

2. What is the name of the subdivision where Uncle Brigham lives?

   _____

3. Which way do you turn onto Kickin' Chicken Drive?

   _____

Word Work

Amelia Earhart Word Search

```
x h n o i t a n i c s a f z
s y y r u b z q j w q i m t
p c t x n r u d p m v b t z
t a w t v z l r w o l w e u
f r w o i q e m c e o k s l
b f e s t w d b g m w t b e
q r x k g m c e o x d k v x
t a s f y b n f c a f i a o
p w y x w d p h r h s y t z
w e y z d p o o e n s i c n
q n a d n s e h e r h m n x
d a t t e m p t n x p t q o
j m h f e b x i b i m a v g
u f k t p e z g x w u g k j
```

Word Bank		
legend	witty	fascination
extensive	trek	attempt

www.summerbridgeactivities.com

The Yew Tree
By Ruedigar Matthes

Murchadh is pronounced: MOOR-uh-choo

Have you ever discovered something by accident?

It was a cold, rainy day in Scotland during early spring of 1787. Finlay, a twelve-year-old boy with messy red hair, was walking with his friend, a tall, scraggly haired lad named Munro.

"I'm glad your uncle let you leave the house this morning. Usually he's in a horrible mood!" said Munro.

Finlay only shrugged. Being an orphan, he had lived with many different uncles and aunts. None of them had really welcomed him, and he never stayed long in one place.

"It's too bad you can't just stay with us," Munro said, but Finlay was storming ahead. He reached the edge of the Brora River and began to slide down the bank.

The river flowed fast with the spring flood, and the swift current was stronger than any man could swim against. As Finlay reached the bottom of the bank, he slipped on a moss-covered rock and fell head-long into the frigid water. He landed with a splash, hitting hit his head on a sharp rock. The water grew red, and Finlay's mind went blank. Munro had seen him slip, but could not make it to help him in time. Finlay was gone.

Finlay woke to a small lamb licking his face and a throbbing headache. He pushed the lamb away and sat up and rubbed his head. It still bled a little from the fall. The rain had stopped, and everything was coated in a layer of impenetrable fog. Finlay looked around at the barely visible countryside trying to figure out where he was, but he had never seen the green, sheep-covered hills that surrounded him. Stranger still, the river was nowhere to be found.

"Where am I?" he wondered as he climbed to his feet. "What has happened?"

"Hello, lad," said a thin, raspy voice. "You should be careful now, for your head has a large bump, as well as a deep cut. When I found you, you were soaked from head to toe, lying in a pile of mossy river wood on the river's bank. Might I ask what happened, and where you came from?"

"I...uh...come from Glenugie, sir," said Finlay. "I don't really remember what happened. It all happened so fast. The last thing I remember is storming into the Brora. Where am I? And who are you?"

"You are in Dalwhinnie and I am called Murchadh, a shepherd. And who might you be?"

"I am called Finlay. I was awakened by one of your sheep. Its tongue was moving over my face like a wild rabbit!"

"Ha! Ha! So you have met Tongue, the smallest sheep in my flock? Well, since you are now up and awake, perhaps you would like a nice bowl of mutton stew?"

"I'm starving. I'll accept your offer of stew and perhaps some dryer clothes, if that isn't too much to ask, good sir."

"Follow me." Murchadh said, walking into the fog. "You know, I have been a shepherd for as long as I can remember, but I don't recall ever finding a nearly drowned person before," he chuckled. "I guess there's a first for everything."

(to be continued)

© RBP Books   www.summerbridgeactivities.com   Reading Connection—Grade 5—RBP0202

Uncovering Ideas

1. How did Finlay get lost in the first part of this story?

   _____

2. Finlay woke up to a strange surprise. What was it?

   _____

3. Describe Murchadh.

   _____

   _____

Connecting to Life

1. This story is about a boy who falls in a river and is taken to a different land. If you could choose to go down a river to another land, where would you want to end up?

   _____

   _____

   _____

2. Predict what will happen in the next part of the story.

   _____

   _____

   _____

Reading Skills Builder

Signal words are words that tell you *when* and *in what order* things happen in the story. Read these sentences and circle the words that show time or when something happened.

Yesterday, I found a kitten in the alley. She was wet and scared. By the next day, she had begun to relax. Just last week, I was thinking about adopting a cat. Now I have a cute kitty. I'll begin looking for its owner tomorrow. Maybe by next week she will truly belong to me.

Circle the words that show the order in which something happened.

Before I went to the store to buy some cookies, I found my allowance money. At the store, first I found my favorite brand of cookies, then brought them to the checkout line. Next, I paid the lady for the cookies. After that, I left the store and walked home. Later in the day, my little sister found my cookies and ate them all. The next day, she felt sick. Serves her right.

Word Work

Often you can change the meaning of a word by adding a **suffix** or **prefix**.

The suffix **-less** means "without." Adding *-less* changes the meaning of the word completely. What do these words mean?

1. aimless: _____ **without aim** _____

2. harmless: _____

3. careless: _____

4. fearless: _____

The prefix **sub-** means "below," as in *subway*, which goes below the ground. Circle the correct answer.

5. A subordinate thing is _____ something else
   a. above   b. in order   c. below

6. A submarine moves _____ the water.
   a. to the side   b. across   c. below

Write four other words that have the prefix **sub-** in them. Use the dictionary if you need to.

7. _____

8. _____

9. _____

10. _____

The Yew Tree (continued)

By Ruedigar Matthes

As Finlay followed Murchadh, he soon noticed a stone hut with a thatched roof barely visible through the soupy fog. Dark smoke swirled from the chimney. They reached the hut and stepped into its warmth. Finlay smelled a rich broth simmering over the fire that crackled in a small stone fireplace. A low bed with a wool blanket lay against the far wall. The room also held a table and chair.

"Smells good," said Finlay, warming his hands by the fire.

"Here are some dry clothes for you, lad."

"Thank you," said Finlay as he grabbed the clothes. He changed into a sheepskin shirt and plaid kilt, which were quite a bit too big, for they had not been made for a child. Finlay sat down at the table and waited for his stew. Murchadh soon placed the steaming bowl before him, and Finlay ate ravenously, as if he hadn't eaten for days. When he was finished, he pushed the bowl away.

Murchadh began to speak again. "It looks as though you will be spending the night here with me, for it will soon be dark, but I will make room…" He looked around his humble home and smiled. "Somewhere." He began to laugh a deep, hearty laugh.

Finlay glanced out the door and saw the bright, orange-red sunset outside like a painted canvas. "Thank you for everything," he said nervously as he realized he was going to arrive back at his home late. His uncle hated it when he was late. "But I really must get going. I must be home before it gets dark. My uncle will be furious if I'm much later. Thank you again." He stood up and hastily headed out the door into the moist air.

"Finlay!" yelled Murchadh. "Finlay! I insist you stay here for the night. The countryside is dangerous, especially for young lads like yourself." But Finlay didn't hear Murchadh's desperate cries, for he was already a long way down the path.

He found a small dirt path that cut through the hillside like a scar and began to follow it. The sun sunk like a stone behind the last hill, and the countryside grew dark. Finlay became frightened.

"You will be fine," he said aloud, trying to reassure himself. "There is nothing to be afraid of."

Just then, he felt as though something had heard him. Finlay looked into the dark and saw two bright, glowing green eyes and heard a low growling. They were the eyes of a fox, a hungry fox. Without thinking, Finlay ran back towards Murchadh's home. The fox followed on his heels. Finlay darted off the path into a grove of trees. He climbed the smallest tree he could find—a dead yew tree—far above the fox's reach. The fox paced around the foot of the tree for a time, then turned and jogged away. Finlay's breathing slowed down, and he relaxed. Just to be sure he had escaped the fox, he decided to stay put for awhile. Soon, a full moon came out, and Finlay fell asleep to the soft gurgling of a nearby stream.   *(to be continued)*

Uncovering Ideas

1. Describe what Murchadh's home is like.

   _____

   _____

2. Rewrite part of this story from where Finlay wakes by the river. Fill in the blanks with your own ideas, not ones from the story.

   What wakes Finlay at the river?

   _____

   Whom does he meet after that?

   _____

   _____

   What happens to him next?

   _____

   _____

On a separate piece of paper, write a two-paragraph version of this part of "The Yew Tree," using your own ideas from above.

Connecting to Life

1. Think about the ways that Murchadh helped Finlay. How have you, or someone you know, been helped in a time of need?

   _____

   _____

2. Think about another story you have heard in which things or places in the story were magical. In 3–5 sentences, explain the story.

   _____

   _____

   _____

   _____

_____

_____

Reading Skills Builder

Outline Finlay's journey.

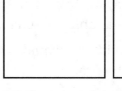

Finlay falls into the river.		
		Finlay climbs the yew tree.

Word Work

Yew Tree Word Search

```
d o y f o o g d t c e m
l v d d c x u e l h d o
e u g n o t r h a t i s
n r l w q q g c d c a s
t h g s h b l a n m l y
g a t z x x i d n c p i
n s n o g z n a o a b v
b k z g r p g e t n d l
y q m t l b j h t v r k
s l o b b e r t u a r v
y m n r n l d p m s l t
s u o i r u f x a k s y
```

Word Bank

broth	canvas	lad
slobber	furious	gurgling
plaid	tangled	mutton
mossy	headache	tongue

By Ruedigar Matthes

While he slept, Finlay dreamed of the strangest happenings. He dreamed that the yew tree had curled around his body and kept him warm. In the night wind, he thought he heard a voice as deep as the ocean whispering a secret into his ears. It was the secret to finding the most wonderful treasures. When he woke, he was still curled up in the yew tree. The fog had cleared, and the sun was shining brightly.

Finlay looked around him. He felt like he was still in a dream, a strange but wonderful dream. The world looked different. A hundred birds sang from the trees, and the sky was a new shade of blue. The world was alive here. Finlay wanted to stay under that sky forever. Somehow, the river had taken him to a place that he knew now he never wanted to leave.

"I will go live with Murchadh," he said aloud.

At this, he climbed down from the tangled branches of the tree and ran back to the dirt path toward Murchadh's home. As he walked, though, his heart began to fill with doubt.

"Murchadh is a poor man," he thought. "And I am a stranger. I would be a burden to him, as I am to my uncle."

As he walked through the grove of trees, he found the stream he had heard the previous night. The cold water felt like drops of heaven; he drank to his heart's content. After quenching his thirst, he noticed a strange, bright-colored rock. He plucked it from the ever-moving stream. It was heavy for its size. He placed the odd rock in his pocket and began to walk back toward the path. As he walked, a plan formed in his mind. After nearly an hour, he spotted Murchadh's house. He began to run as fast as his skinny legs could carry

him. He burst through the door, almost bursting it off the hinges.

"My, my, what seems to be the problem, Finlay?" Murchadh said as he stopped chopping potatoes.

"I want to stay and live with you. I will be a shepherd, and I will work very hard. I promise," Finlay said, still out of breath. He looked cautiously into Murchadh's eyes, hoping the old shepherd would let him stay.

"I thought you were going home."

Finlay related the story of his night in the yew tree. By the time he finished, Murchadh knew what had happened.

"There is a legend of a man who climbed the branches of the yew tree one night under a full moon and never came down," said the shepherd. "To this day, the yew tree is a place of magic. The man became a part of that tree. It is said that if you climb the yew tree under a full moon, and stay awhile, the man will whisper in your ear. They say he will tell you which way to go to find luck."

"Maybe it was meant to be. Maybe the yew tree told you to come help a poor shepherd who is getting too old to tend his own sheep." With that, Murchadh told Finlay he could stay. Finlay embraced the old man and felt the stone he had found in the stream earlier.

"When I was down by the stream getting a water, I found this odd rock," he said, pulling the bright stone from his pocket.

"My goodness! Lad, this is gold!" The shepherd looked into Finlay's eyes. "The man did tell you where to find luck."

Murchadh and Finlay began to laugh. Murchadh put his arm on Finlay's shoulder, and the two walked out into the day. For the first time in as long as he could remember, Finlay felt hope—and he knew the real luck he had found.

www.summerbridgeactivities.com

Uncovering Ideas

1. What is the legend of the yew tree?

   _____

   _____

   _____

2. Choose the best answer for how Finlay felt when he woke up in the yew tree.

   a. He was tired and his back was sore.
   b. He saw the world in a new way.
   c. He was afraid the fox would come back and eat him.
   d. He was craving Murchadh's McMutton Burgers.

3. What statement best states the moral (or main lesson) of this story?

   a. Never fall asleep in a yew tree.
   b. Don't walk in a river alone.
   c. A fox in a tree is worth two on the ground.
   d. Luck can find you even if you're not looking.

Connecting to Life

1. A legend is a story that is told over and over that may or may not be true. What is an example of a legend you have heard? (Many times people who tell legends start off by saying, "This really happened, or this happened to a friend of mine.")

   _____

   _____

   _____

2. If you could climb into the yew tree, what do you think it would whisper to you?

   _____

   _____

Reading Skills Builder

Corvallis Happenings Guide: Local Information, Table of Contents

1. On what page of the guide would you find what kind of fast-food places are in town? _____

2. On what page would there be information about what the weather is like? _____

3. You want to see if there are any good movies playing; what page would you look under? _____

4. You want to see if there are any job openings; what page would you look under? _____

5. You want a copy of the bus schedule; what page would you find it on? _____

Word Work

An **adjective** is a word that describes a noun. A **noun** is person, place, or thing. In the phrase "strange dream," *strange* is an adjective because it tells what kind of dream it was. Underline the adjectives in the sentences below.

1. The colorful rock fell out of my pocket.

2. It was a cool night.

3. The boy had skinny legs.

4. The old shepherd gave the boy some stew.

5. Please turn off the hot water.

6. He climbed down the tangled branches.

7. The red fox ran through the woods.

My Cherry Tree House
By Kristen Diebele

White Sands
By Matt Kendell

Are there discoveries to be made in your own backyard?

On Location: My Backyard

I yawned and wiped the sleep from my eyes as I looked at my surroundings. I didn't want to leave the warmth the couch had absorbed from my body. I got up reluctantly, almost collapsing, but that funny fuzzy feeling soon left my legs, fading out through my toes into the carpet.

I let out one good sigh and had one good stretch. Then I was ready to start my day.

My goal that morning was the large cherry tree in the center of my yard. It was my special place away from the world. It had a tree house built strong by my grandpa. I climbed the rusty ladder made of metal pipes. My hands turned reddish-orange from the worn ladder. I wiped the rust on my pants and kept climbing.

I steadied myself, then sat down in the tree house. I gazed at the ripe cherries, swollen with juice, ready to burst like fat little balloons. Usually the cherries were gone because the blue jays would eat them, but there were many cherries left. I thought the birds must have slept in.

The branches drooped heavy with cherries, and I stretched to reach one. I swung it back and forth, picturing the pendulum of a clock in my mind. My tongue felt around my mouth for a tooth chipped from biting into a cherry last summer. I leaned over and squeezed the cherry until the slimy pit fell to the ground beneath the tree. Then I lay back to look at the morning …

I am now 13 years old. The tree house grew old and rotten; it fell to

> *The real voyage of discovery consists not in seeking new landscapes, but in having new eyes.*
> —Marcel Proust

the ground. My grandfather, who built the tree house, died from cancer. Things have changed, and so have I. You may think because my tree house has fallen, that I have lost my special place, but you're wrong. My tree house and my grandpa are both in a special place in my mind. It's someplace I can go wherever I am.

On Location: White Sands National Monument

The sand dunes look like snow-covered hills with plants sticking out. People can climb up or sled down many of the dunes. If you look closely, the sand looks like salt. It is made from a mineral called gypsum, and it is rarely found like this. Usually it is mixed with rainwater and washed out to sea.

In parts of the dunes are wood paths that have signs telling about the plants and animals that live there. Lots of plants live in these sand dunes. One plant, called the yucca, holds the sand around it in place with its roots. The wind blows the sand away, but some stays stuck in the roots and looks like a stump.

Many animals live amongst the dunes. Sometimes you can see a lizard hiding under a bush or running away from people. There are also coyotes, rabbits, and foxes, for example. Most of them hide in burrows during the day to keep themselves from overheating. Many animals have adopted a white color to help them blend in. It's hard for plants and animals to live in the dunes because their home in the sand keeps being moved by the wind. In fact, at first glance you might not think anything lived here at all. But if you look closely, you might be surprised at what you see.

© RBP Books   www.summerbridgeactivities.com   Reading Connection—Grade 5—RBP0202

Uncovering Ideas

1. How can the tree house in the cherry tree still be a special place to the author even though it is gone?

   _____

   _____

   _____

2. What kinds of animals live in the sand dunes, and how do they live?

   _____

   _____

   _____

3. If you could choose to be in a cherry tree or play in the sand dunes right now, which would you choose? Why?

   _____

   _____

   _____

Connecting to Life

1. Draw a map of your neighborhood. Draw natural landmarks: trees, ponds, a canal, etc. After you finish, circle a spot on your map that holds special memories for you.

   Write why you choose to focus on that place. Describe that place in words.

   +--+
   | |
   | |
   | |
   | |
   | |
   | |
   | |
   | |
   +--+

_____

_____

Reading Skills Builder

Which of the following resources would you look in to find out how far Boise, Idaho, is from Salt Lake City, Utah?

a. _____ a thesaurus

b. _____ an encyclopedia

c. _____ *Guinness Book of World Records*

d. _____ a map of the United States

Word Work

Think about the following phrases from the writing. Use one or two of the phrases to make up your own poem or a small story.

1. washed out to sea
2. chipped tooth
3. stuck in the roots
4. ripe cherries
5. funny fuzzy feeling
6. fat little balloons

_____

_____

_____

_____

_____

_____

_____

Honey Lovin' Stories

By Anna Hanks

Talking to your parents and grandparents can be a great way to discover your own history. In this bit of family folklore, the author talks about her mother's life as a beekeeper's daughter.

I come from honey-loving, beekeeping people. My Grandpa Hal Hanks worked as a beekeeper in a small town in Idaho, a place that smells like sagebrush and is so small that cows outnumber people.

His five children helped him in the beekeeping business. They would come home with sticky hands and bee stings on their ankles and wherever else the pesky bugs could make their mark. Because my grandpa died young, I have never heard any beekeeping stories from his own lips. So I asked my mom to tell me her stories. They were undiluted and fresh, like raw honey from a comb. Listening to her stories was sweet, like tasting a bit of history dripping from a honey knife.

In these stories, my mother talks about some of the medicinal uses of honey by her family.

Sucking Warm Honey from the Comb

"When I was young, I had asthma. It was so bad that at night I couldn't lie down to sleep. One thing that helped me was to take fresh beeswax and honeycomb with the warm honey still in it and just chew it. That would open my nasal passages so that I could relax and breathe better. I had a lot of allergies to pollens and sagebrush (we lived in a desert, so that didn't help) and to the cottonwood trees by our house."

Baby Soft

"Every year, Dad sold his beeswax from the honey crop that he got. He would melt it down and sell it to companies who used it to make lipstick, lotion, and other cosmetics. One of the values of beeswax and honey was softening your hands. It would soften everything it touched.

"As we worked in the shop uncapping the wax from the honeycomb and using the extractor to spin the honey out of the hives, our gloves became coated with honey and wax. We had a bucket of water we kept dipping them in because they'd get so sticky they'd stick to the machinery. We kept our hands in honey water all day long. Rather quickly, our hands would become just as soft as a baby's skin."

Bee Stings for Bowling Knees

"One of the hobbies that Grandpa loved was bowling. But he had arthritis in his knees, and it was painful to bowl. So before he went bowling, he would get some bees in a bottle, bring them into the house, and force the bees to sting him on either side of his knee. We laughed about it because it hurt to have that done. He would actually pick up the bee and kind of place it there, and make it angry, so it would stick its stinger in. The bee venom had something in it that would allow the knee to work freely. Grandpa would be free of his arthritis so that he could go bowling."

www.summerbridgeactivities.com   Reading Connection—Grade 5—RBP0202

Uncovering Ideas

1. This story is an example of

   a. fiction

   b. folklore

   c. a legend

   d. poetry

2. Under each column, write down what the story said that honey did for the following health problems.

asthma	dry skin	arthritis

Connecting to Life

1. Imagine that you are going to interview a grandparent or older person about their life when they were younger. Write a list of six questions you would ask them.

   _____

   _____

   _____

   _____

   _____

   _____

Reading Skills Builder

Look at the following advertisement, and answer the questions below.

Nestled in the heart of small-town Idaho lives Hal Hanks, the man who knows the secret to delicious honey: happy bees. Hal Hanks, owner of Hanks Honey, has been keeping bees for 30 years. The folks in town say he treats his bees like gold; he even sings them to sleep. Mr. Hanks collects the bees' sweet nectar when it's fresh from the honeycomb. Hanks Honey is not diluted like other brands—it's straight from the bee to you. So stick with Grandpa Hanks' honey, sweet and country-fresh. There's a bit of heaven in every drop!

1. How many years has the beekeeper been keeping bees?

   _____

2. What state does Hanks' honey come from?

   _____

3. According to the advertisement, what's one thing that is special about Hanks' honey?

   _____

   _____

Word Work

Put the following words in one of the columns below, depending on if the word has to do with honey or with bees.

dripping	raw	pesky	angry
fresh	buzzing	sweet	noisy

honey	bees

A Bird Came Down the Walk

By Emily Dickinson

Have you ever dreamt of being famous?

Emily Dickinson published only seven poems while she was alive. After Emily died, her sister discovered about 1,700 poems Emily had written on scraps of paper, envelopes, and paper bags, all tied into little packages. Now Emily Dickinson is one of the most famous early American poets. Before you read her poem, write your own version by putting in words that you choose from the word bank into the blanks below.

Word Bank

drank	ocean	saw
beads	butterflies	dew
crumb	eyes	bird
grass	angle-worm	home
beetle	walk	feathers
oars	swim	hopped
head	awkward	ate
glanced	beak	one

A _____ came down the _____

He did not know I _____;

He bit an _____ in halves

And ate the fellow, raw.

And then he _____ a _____

From a convenient _____,

And then _____ sidewise to the wall

To let a _____ pass.

He _____ with rapid _____

That hurried all abroad,—

They looked like frightened _____, I thought;

He stirred his velvet _____.

Like _____ in danger, cautious,

I offered him a _____,

And he unrolled his _____

And rowed him softer _____

Than _____ divide the _____,

Too silver for a seam,

Or _____, off banks of noon,

Leap, plashless as they _____.

Leap, plashless as they swim.

Or Butterflies, off Banks of Noon,

Too silver for a seam—

Than Oars divide the Ocean,

And rowed him softer home—

And he unrolled his feathers

I offered him a Crumb,

Like one in danger, Cautious,

He stirred his velvet head

thought—

They looked like frightened Beads, I

That hurried all abroad—

He glanced with rapid eyes

To let a Beetle pass—

And then hopped sidewise to the Wall

From a convenient Grass,

And then he drank a Dew

And ate the fellow, raw,

He bit an angle-worm in halves

He did not know I saw—

A Bird Came down the Walk—

Uncovering Ideas

1. What is Emily Dickinson's poem about?

   _____

   _____

   _____

2. The person who is writing the poem is

   a. watching a snake

   b. gardening

   c. watching a bird

   d. reading a book

Connecting to Life

1. In the space below, draw a picture of what you see the bird doing in this poem.

Reading Skills Builder

Jonah is looking for books by some of his favorite authors in the library. He knows that all fiction books are organized according to the last name of the author.

Put these books in alphabetical order by the last name of the author.

___ *The Giver* by Lois Lowry

___ *Mossflower* (Red Wall Series) by Brian Jacques

___ *Hatchet* by Gary Paulsen

___ *James and the Giant Peach* by Roald Dahl

___ *The Hobbit* by J.R.R. Tolkien

Word Work

Below is a list of homonyms. **Homonyms** are words that sound the same but are spelled differently and have different meanings.

Write three sentences, using a pair of homonyms in each sentence.

billed	build
bored	board
cell	sell
flour	flower
hour	our
knight	night
meat	meet

1. _____

   _____

2. _____

   _____

3. _____

   _____

Contractions are words that join together two small words by adding an apostrophe ('). Write the contractions for the words below:

1. you are _____

2. they are _____

3. we are _____

4. is not _____

5. were not _____

6. are not _____

Frankenstein

By Mary Shelley, *adapted*

At times, what we discover is not what we had hoped to find. The story Frankenstein *is about a man who spends years working on a project only to find that the finished product is nothing like what he had imagined. Have you ever created something that didn't turn out the way you wanted it to? How did you feel about it?*

It was on a dreary night of November that I saw what I had created. With terrible fear, I collected the instruments of life around me to bring life to the thing that lay at my feet. It was already one in the morning. The rain pattered gloomily against the panes, and my candle was nearly burnt out, when, in the dim light, I saw the dull yellow eye of the creature open. It breathed hard, and its limbs began to move.

How can I describe my emotions when seeing the creature that I, with such pain and care, had tried to create? I had tried to make his features beautiful. His yellow skin barely covered the muscles and veins beneath; his hair was of a lustrous black, and flowing; his teeth of a pearly whiteness. But these features only formed a more horrible contrast with his watery eyes, that seemed almost of the same color as the eye sockets in which they were set, and his shrunken face and straight black lips.

I had worked hard for nearly two years to put life into an inanimate body. For this I had deprived myself of rest and health. It had been all I wanted, but now that I had finished, the beauty of the dream vanished, and sickness filled my heart. Unable to face the man I had created, I rushed out of the room and started walking back and forth in my bedroom, unable to sleep.

I threw myself on the bed in my clothes, but I could not relax. I slept, but had the wildest dreams. I thought I saw Elizabeth, healthy and happy, walking in the streets of Ingolstadt. Surprised, I hugged her, but as I kissed her lips, her face began to change. I woke up in horror. A cold dew covered my forehead, my teeth chattered, and my body shook.

Then, by the dim and yellow light of the moon, I beheld the miserable monster that I had created. He held up the curtain of the bed, and his eyes looked at me. His jaws opened, and he made some sounds, while a grin wrinkled his cheeks. One hand was stretched out, to hold me back, but I escaped and rushed downstairs. I hid in the courtyard and stayed there for rest of the night, walking up and down, listening closely, fearing each sound as if it were to announce the devil I had given life to. Oh! No one can imagine the horror of that face. Oh! A mummy brought back to life could not be so hideous. I had looked at him while unfinished, and he was ugly then, but when those muscles and joints began to move, it was even more horrible.

I passed the night wretchedly. Sometimes my pulse beat so quickly that I felt the beating in every vein. Sometimes, I nearly sank to the ground through weakness. I also felt terribly disappointed; my dreams had become a curse to me.

(to be continued)

www.summerbridgeactivities.com   **Reading Connection—Grade 5—RBP0202**

Uncovering Ideas

1. On a separate sheet of paper, draw a picture of what you think Frankenstein's monster looks like. Use details from the story to help you draw the picture.

2. How did the man in the story feel about his creation? Use examples from the story to back up what you think.

   _____

   _____

3. What time period do you think the story is based in? Use examples from the story to back up your ideas.

   _____

   _____

Connecting to Life

1. Write about a time that you created or built something that didn't turn out the way you thought it would. Example: something you cooked, or built, or put together. How did you feel about how it turned out?

   _____

   _____

   _____

   _____

2. Tell what you would do if you had created the monster.

   _____

   _____

   _____

   _____

Reading Skills Builder

1. Where in the library would you find out how to bake an angel food cake?

   a. A book on what angels eat

   b. A thesaurus

   c. *Betty Crocker's Guide to Rollerblading in the West*

   d. *The Joy of Cooking*

Word Work

The answers to this crossword puzzle use words that have the "j" sound but are spelled with a *g*. For example: *gym*.

G-word Crossword Puzzle

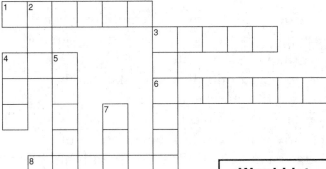

Word List
huge
biology
danger
gibberish
giant
message
gem
gym
manage
age

Across

1. to take care of something
3. uses a tree as a toothpick
4. valuable part of a ring
6. study of life
8. You want to avoid this.

Down

2. what you do to get older
3. crazy talking
4. basketball lover's hangout
5. what answering machines love to get
7. the opposite of *tiny*

By Mary Shelley, *adapted*

Morning came, depressing and wet. I began pacing the streets with quick steps, wanting to avoid the monster that I feared would be at every turn in the street. I did not dare go back to my apartment, but hurried on, drenched by the rain, which poured from a black and comfortless sky. I walked the streets with no idea of where I was or what I was doing. My heart was sick with fear, and I hurried on, not daring to look around me.

Finally, I came to an inn where carriages usually stop. Here I stopped, not knowing why. I remained there watching a coach that was coming towards me from the other end of the street. It stopped just where I was standing, and as the door was opened, I saw Henry Clerval.

"My dear Frankenstein," he said, "How glad I am to see you! How lucky that you should be here, the same time as I arrive!" I was so happy to see Clerval. I suddenly forgot about my worries and fear, and felt, for the first time during many months, calm and happiness. I welcomed my friend, and we walked towards my home.

As we walked, he told me how he had finally convinced his father to let him go to college. We also talked about how worried my father and Elizabeth had been.

Then, he said looking straight into my face, "I did not before tell you how very ill you appear; so thin and pale; you look as if you had been watching for several nights."

"You have guessed right; I have lately been working so hard on something, that I haven't had enough rest; but I hope that my work is now finished, and I can be free."

I walked quickly, and we soon arrived at my rooms. I then I began to think about whether the creature I had left in my apartment might still be there. I dreaded to see this monster, but I was more afraid that Henry should see him. I convinced him to stay a few minutes at the bottom of the stairs, and I darted up towards my own room. My hand was already on the lock of the door before I pulled myself together. I paused, and a cold shivering came over me. I threw the door open, but nothing appeared. I stepped fearfully in: the apartment was empty. I could hardly believe that I had been so lucky. I clapped my hands for joy and ran down to Clerval. We ascended into my room, and the servant brought breakfast; but I couldn't contain myself. I jumped over the chairs, clapped my hands, and laughed aloud. Clerval at first thought I was just happy to see him, but when he looked more closely, he saw a wildness in my eyes.

"My dear Victor," cried he, "what's the matter? What is the cause of all this?"

"Do not ask me," I said, putting my hands in front of my eyes, for I thought I saw the dreaded creature come into the room.

"Oh, save me! Save me!" I imagined that the monster grabbed me. I struggled and fell down in a fit. Poor Clerval! He had been looking forward to spending time with me, and his happiness turned to sadness. But I could not even see his sadness because my body had turned lifeless and did not recover for a long, long time.

Uncovering Ideas

1. Why do you think the man in the story went mad?

   _____

   _____

   _____

2. In three words, describe the mood of the main character in this story.

   _____

   _____

3. Write three questions that you would ask the main character in this story.

   _____

   _____

   _____

   _____

Connecting to Life

1. Have you ever created, cooked, or built something that didn't turn out the way you had hoped it would? Write about what happened.

   _____

   _____

   _____

   _____

   _____

Reading Skills Builder

Read the information below from the box of Corn Krisps, and answer the questions.

Ingredients: Corn, wheat bran, sugar, corn syrup, salt, wheat flour, molasses, malted barley flour, BHT added to preserve freshness

Hope Foods, Inc.
Box 4090
Emerald City, Kansas 90044

1. What is the second ingredient in Corn Krisps?

   _____

2. What is added to the cereal to preserve freshness?

   _____

3. Where is Hope Foods located?

   _____

4. How many ingredients are in Corn Krisps?

   _____

Word Work

Antonyms are words that have opposite meanings. Match the **antonyms** in these lists.

healthy	peace
happy	down
friend	play
war	sick
in	enemy
up	sad
work	hot
cold	out

"Humpty Dumpty" from *Through the Looking-Glass*

By Lewis Carroll

Have you ever read a poem you couldn't understand?

"Let's hear it," said Humpty Dumpty. "I can explain all the poems that ever were invented—and a good many that haven't been invented just yet."

This sounded very hopeful, so Alice repeated the first verse:

"'Twas brillig, and the slithy toves
Did gyre and gimble in the wabe;
All mimsy were the borogoves,
And the mome raths outgrabe."

"That's enough to begin with," Humpty Dumpty interrupted: "there are plenty of hard words there. '*Brillig*' means four o'clock in the afternoon—the time when you begin *broiling* things for dinner."

"That'll do very well," said Alice: "and '*slithy*'?"

"Well, '*slithy*' means 'lithe and slimy.' 'Lithe' is the same as 'active.' You see it's like a portmanteau—there are two meanings packed up into one word."

"I see it now," Alice remarked thoughtfully: "and what are '*toves*'?"

"Well, '*toves*' are something like badgers—they're something like lizards—and they're something like corkscrews."

"They must be very curious creatures."

"They are that," said Humpty Dumpty: "also, they make their nests under sundials—also they live on cheese."

"And what's to '*gyre*' and to '*gimble*'?"

"To '*gyre*' is to go round and round like a gyroscope. To '*gimble*' is to make holes like a gimlet."

"And '*the wabe*' is the grass-plot round a sundial, I suppose?" said Alice, surprised at her own ingenuity.

"Of course it is. It's called '*wabe*,' you know, because it goes a long way before it, and a long way behind it—"

"And a long way beyond it on each side," Alice added.

"Exactly so. Well, then '*mimsy*' is 'flimsy and miserable' (there's another portmanteau for you). And a '*borogove*' is a thin shabby-looking bird with its feathers sticking out all round—something like a live mop."

"And then '*mome raths*'?" said Alice. "If I'm not giving you too much trouble."

"Well, a '*rath*' is a sort of green pig: but '*mome*' I'm not certain about. I think it's short for 'from home'—meaning that they'd lost their way, you know."

"And what does '*outgrabe*' mean?"

"Well, '*outgrabing*' is something between bellowing and whistling, with a kind of sneeze in the middle: however, you'll hear it done, maybe—down in the wood yonder—and when you've once heard it you'll be *quite* content. Who's been repeating all that hard stuff to you?"

"I read it in a book," said Alice. "But I had some poetry repeated to me, much easier than that, by—Tweedledee, I think."

"As to poetry, you know," said Humpty Dumpty, stretching out one of his great hands, "*I* can repeat poetry as well as other folk if it comes to that—"

"Oh, it needn't come to that!" Alice hastily said, hoping to keep him from beginning.

Uncovering Ideas

1. What word did Humpty Dumpty say means a "shabby-looking bird with its feathers sticking out, like a live mop"?

    _____

2. In Humpty Dumpty's opinion, what is a *mome rath*?

    a. a yellow chicken that is homesick

    b. an angry fruit salad

    c. a green pig that has lost its way

    d. the grass plot around a sun dial

3. Using Humpty Dumpty's definitions, translate this part of the poem:

    'Twas brillig and the slithy toves
    Did gyre and gimble in the wabe.

    _____

    _____

    _____

    _____

Connecting to Life

1. What do you do when you come across a word in a book that you don't know?

    _____

    _____

2. Find two words in this book that you don't know. Guess what they mean. Then use your dictionary to check your guess.

    Word 1 _____

    Guess 1 _____

    Answer 1 _____

    Word 2 _____

    Guess 2 _____

    Answer 2 _____

Reading Skills Builder

Pretend you were assigned to interview the author of this story for a newspaper article. Write down five questions that you would ask him about himself and why he writes the way he does.

1. _____

    _____

2. _____

    _____

3. _____

    _____

4. _____

    _____

5. _____

    _____

Word Work

Make up your own crazy words to replace the words in parentheses in this short paragraph:

> It was (a day of week) during the (a season) and the (color) (animal) (bug) did (an action) in (a place).

Rewrite the paragraph with your new words.

_____

_____

_____

_____

_____

_____

John Colter, Western Explorer

By Joe Soderborg

What part of the world would you most like to explore?

John Colter died at a young age, but before he did, he saw and explored more American wilderness than nearly any man of his time. He was one of the first Americans to cross the continent and see the Pacific Ocean. He traveled through territory full of hostile Indians. He saw amazing natural wonders that no American had seen before. The stories he told about his adventures were so fantastic that people didn't believe him.

John Colter was born about 1774 in Virginia. In 1803, he set off into the unknown wilderness of the American West. He traveled with a group called the "Corps of Discovery." The Corps included 31 other men, a teenage girl, and a little baby. Their goal was to find a water-way that would connect the Missouri River and the Pacific Ocean. Two army captains named Lewis and Clark were the group's leaders. The Corps suffered hardship, hunger, sickness, and fatigue, but the journey made them famous.

After nearly two years in the wilderness, the Corps of Discovery was headed back to St. Louis, Missouri. As they neared a Mandan Indian village in what is now South Dakota, they met a company of fur trappers coming up the Missouri River. The company was eager for information about the wilderness, so John Colter decided to stay and be their guide.

On one of his trips to trap for furs, John came across the strangest landscape he had ever seen. Water boiled from the earth and shot seventy feet into the air. Thick mud bubbled from stinking pools and filled the air with a foul stench. All kinds of wild animals roamed freely through this land of strange beauty.

Colter had wandered into an area the local Indians called "Land of Fire." Today we call the area Yellowstone National Park. People who heard his amazing stories of Yellowstone thought Colter made them up. Because of his descriptions of boiling pools and steam coming from the earth, people called this place Colter's Hell.

John Colter lived a life of adventure. But how did he die? Did he fall with an arrow in his chest? Did he die in the harsh elements of the wild? His death was neither violent nor heroic. Colter was living on an Iowa farm in 1812 when he died in his bed of a disease called jaundice.

www.summerbridgeactivities.com

Uncovering Ideas

1. John Colter was part of a group of explorers called the

   ____ Corps of Discovery

   ____ Eastern Tour De West

   ____ Riders of the Blue Sage

   ____ Rocky Mountaineers

2. Name one thing that Colter discovered on his journey.

   _____

   _____

3. Why do you think some people didn't believe Colter's stories about the land around Yellowstone?

   _____

   _____

Connecting to Life

1. Imagine that you could be the first person to discover a wilderness place. What place would you want to discover?

   _____

   _____

2. Pretend you are John Colter and are writing about your discoveries in your journal. Write one day's events. Be descriptive as you write about what you see.

Feb 18, 1804

Dear Journal,

Today I discovered _____

   _____

   _____

   _____

   _____

_____

_____

Reading Skills Builder

In what order would you expect to find these words in the dictionary?

_____ huckleberry

_____ grizzly bear

_____ buttercup

_____ Yellowstone Park

_____ geyser

_____ expedition

Word Work

John Colter Word Search

```
p m b r e l i t s o h r
h f g e x y e n s z c p
e m a m a x l e e o t y
i a g n p g u n n l n n
d t q l t g e t r v e y
v e o r i a i r e l l h
e r q t v n s q d l o l
e f a m e l a t l o i y
h f l n q j m c i d v x
g c t p i x g w w c n b
e c i d n u a j g y w y
u s y r o t i r r e t g
```

Word Bank

fatigue	hostile	violent
eager	fantastic	wilderness
territory	continent	explore
	jaundice	

John Colter's Escape

By Joseph Soderborg

How do you think you would act in a life or death situation?

John Colter was an explorer who traveled with Lewis and Clark across the continent. He trapped for furs, fought Indians, explored new country, and survived in a harsh wilderness. He became a legend when he escaped from a whole tribe of Blackfoot Indians who chased him for five miles across cactus-covered prairies and sharp volcanic rock.

It happened in 1809 in Wyoming. Blackfoot Indians suddenly surrounded John Colter and his traveling companion, John Potts. The Indians shot Potts and captured Colter. They stripped him naked and held a council to decide his fate. Colter could understand some of their language, and he knew they were discussing how to kill him. The chief asked him "Can you run fast?"

"No," Colter said. But living in the wilderness for years had made him physically fit and vigorous. Besides, he was scared for his life, and the will to live burned within him. The chief had Colter start walking away from the camp. After he had gone a few hundred yards, someone gave a yell, and all of the braves in the camp sprinted after him.

The Yellowstone River was five miles away. Colter knew if he could get to the river he might have a chance. The ground was rough and covered with sharp rocks and prickly pear cacti. The Indians wore thick, leather moc-casins. Colter raced for his life in bare feet! The soles of his feet were soon covered with cactus needles. His lungs felt ready to explode in the thin, mountain air. But he had to run faster; several Indians were gaining on him. He could have given up, but his will to live roared like a great fire within him.

He called up every bit of strength and ener-gy, but after a couple of miles his nose started to bleed profusely. One of the Indians was right behind him, so Colter turned to fight. Colter grabbed the surprised Indian's spear and plunged it into him. He snatched a blanket from the brave's waist and continued running.

At last he reached the river and dove in. The icy water washed away the blood and soothed his torn feet. He hid under a logjam as the braves hunted for him on both sides of the river. The tired trapper stayed in the river until dark, then crawled out to finish his escape. He climbed over a giant moun-tain in the dark and finally stumbled into a trading post a couple of weeks later. His arrival at the trading post led to perhaps the most important discovery he had ever made. It was a discovery about himself.

Although John Colter marched with the Corps of Discovery, blazed trails, explored a vast wilderness, and discov-ered fabulous geysers, his greatest discovery was just how strong the will to live could be.

© RBP Books   www.summerbridgeactivities.com   Reading Connection—Grade 5—RBP0202

Uncovering Ideas

1. Describe the setting where this story takes place. What was the land like?

   _____

   _____

2. What were the Indians planning?

   _____

   _____

3. What questions do you have about this event in history that the author has not included in this brief story?

   _____

   _____

   _____

   _____

Connecting to Life

1. Tell about a time that you were chased.

   _____

   _____

   _____

2. Describe what you would do in John Colter's situation.

   _____

   _____

   _____

   _____

Reading Skills Builder

Outline what happens during the chase.

John Colter is captured...

He makes it alive to the trading post.

Word Work

Escape Word Search

```
o w s m q r a d i z b s d f
p u y n m d y f x j m n e q
r x v j y e t r c s h i r y
o n w x r l e z h o w s u b
f a l b a b t r a o e a t u
u v v p e i r t s t d c p g
s q u c p d w c e h i c a f
e p y i s e v a d e z o c e
l l p n u r v c s d s m h y
y o n a m c t t p h o u z x
t g q c b n k u t c n h f g
w j i l q i d s g t k p x w
d a y o o y x h e g l b x e
i m l v x p h d c l k e f z
```

Word Bank

profusely	incredible	captured
logjam	soothed	moccasins
cactus	spear	hunted
chased	volcanic	

Quotes about Nature

by John Muir

Would you like to live in the mountains for months at a time?

BEARS

"In my first interview with a Sierra bear we were frightened and embarrassed, both of us, but the bear's behavior was better than mine."
Our National Parks, pg. 174

"What digestion! A sheep or a wounded deer or a pig [the bear] eats warm, about as quickly as a boy eats a buttered muffin…"
Our National Parks, pg. 173

"Bears, too, roam this foodful wilderness, feeding on grass, clover, berries, nuts, ant eggs, fish, flesh, or fowl… with but little troublesome discrimination. Sugar and honey they seem to like best of all, and they seek far to find the sweets; but when hard pushed by hunger they make out to gnaw a living from the bark of trees and rotten logs, and might almost live on clean lava alone."
Steep Trails, pg. 27

"Bears are made of the same dust as we, and breathe the same winds and drink the same waters. A bear's days are warmed by the same sun, his dwellings are overdomed by the same blue sky, and his life turns and ebbs with heart-pulsings like ours, and was poured from the same First Fountain."
Wilderness World of John Muir, pg. 313

ESKIMOS

"I heard merry shouting, and looking round, saw a band of Eskimos—men, women and children loose and hairy like wild animals—running towards me. I could not guess at first what they were seeking, for they seldom leave the shore; but soon they told me, as they threw themselves down, sprawling and laughing, on the mellow bog, and began to feast on the berries."
Our National Parks, pg. 9–10

"… it is far safer to wander in God's woods than to travel on black highways or to stay at home."
Our National Parks, pg. 28

LIGHTNING

"If you are not very strong, try to climb Electric Peak (YELLOWSTONE) when a big bossy, well-charged thunder-cloud is on it, to breathe the ozone set free, and get yourself kindly shaken and shocked. You are sure to be lost in wonder and praise, and every hair of your head will stand up and hum and sing like an enthusiastic congrega-tion."

Our National Parks, pg. 59

MOUNTAINS

"One day's exposure to mountains is better than cartloads of books."

"Thousands of God's wild blessings will search you and soak you as if you were a sponge, and the big days will go by uncounted."
Our National Parks, pg. 17

"Climb the mountains and get their good tidings. Nature's peace will flow into you as sunshine flows into trees. The winds will blow their own freshness into you, and the storms their energy, while care will drop off like autumn leaves."
Our National Parks, pg. 56

SUNSET

"…the sun is already in the west, and soon our day will be done."
Our National Parks, pg. 73

www.summerbridgeactivities.com
Reading Connection—Grade 5—RBP0202

Uncovering Ideas

1. Name three things that John Muir says bears like to eat.

   _____

2. What does John Muir mean when he writes: "One day's exposure to mountains is better than a cartload of books." What kind of education do you think the mountains can give you?

   _____

3. John Muir thinks it's safer to walk in the woods than to be at home. Do you agree or disagree with him? Why or why not? Explain your answer.

   _____

   _____

   _____

Connecting to Life

1. What is your favorite place to be in nature? Why?

   _____

   _____

   _____

Reading Skills Builder

You have to call a few people today. Put these names in the order you would find them in the phone book.

_____Alcott, Louisa May

_____King, Martin Luther

_____Presley, Elvis

_____Shakespeare, William

_____Chaplin, Charlie

_____Churchill, Winston

_____Muir, John

Word Work

How good is a piece of plain bread with nothing on it? About as good as a story that doesn't use descriptive words. A good writer gives you creamy butter and berry jam to spread on your bread. Good writers add details and description to flavor their stories. They choose delicious words that are specific and descriptive.

Study these examples and see how John Muir spiced up the description. The first sentence is the Plain Bread Way. Underneath is John Muir's Butter and Jam Writing.

1. The raincloud was powerful.
   "a big bossy, well-charged thunder-cloud"

2. The Eskimos looked wild.
   "the men and women were loose and hairy like wild animals"

3. Nature blesses us.
   "the wild blessings will search and soak you as if you were a sponge"

4. The bears eat bark.
   "they gnaw a living from the bark of trees and rotten logs"

Add descriptions to these boring sentences to make them more interesting.

1. The wind was strong._____

   _____

   _____

2. The river was cold. _____

   _____

   _____

3. Dinner smelled great. _____

   _____

   _____

The Wee Fell Yin (The Little Terror)

Adapted from Sara Cone Bryant, *How to Tell Stories to Children and Some Stories to Tell*

What happens when a country dog moves to the city?

This is a story about a dog, a slim, silky-haired, sharp-eared little dog who was the prettiest thing you can imagine. Her name was Wylie, and she lived in Scotland, far up on the hills, where she helped her master take care of his sheep.

She watched over the little lambs like a soldier and never let anything hurt them. She drove them out to pasture, and when the silly sheep got frightened and ran this way and that, hurting themselves and getting lost, Wylie knew exactly what to do. She would run, barking and scolding, till they were all bunched together in front of the right gate. She loved her work.

At last her master grew too old to stay alone on the hills, and so he went away to live. Before he went, he gave Wylie to two kind young men who lived in a nearby town.

Now Wylie lived in the city where there were no sheep farms, only streets and houses, and she did not have to do any work at all. She was just a pet dog. She seemed very happy, and she was always good.

But after a while, the family noticed something odd about their pet. Every Tuesday night, about nine o'clock, Wylie disappeared. She would be gone all night. But every Wednesday morning, there she was at the door, her silky coat all sweaty and muddy and her feet heavy with weariness, but her bright eyes looked up at her masters as if she were trying to explain where she had been. Week after week the same thing happened, and her masters wondered where in the world did Wylie go?

You never could guess, so I am going to tell you.

In the city near the town where the kind young men lived was a big market. On Tuesday nights, the farmers used to come down from the hills with their sheep to sell. They would drive them through the city streets into the pens, ready for market on Wednesday morning.

The sheep weren't used to the city noises and sights, and they always grew afraid and wild, giving the farmers and the sheepdogs a great deal of trouble. They would break away and run about in everybody's way.

But just as the trouble was worst, about sunrise, the farmers would see a little silky, sharp-eared dog come trotting all alone down the road into the middle of the sheep.

And then!

In and out the little dog ran like the wind, driving, coaxing, pushing, making the sheep mind like a good schoolteacher till they were all safely in! No one knew whose dog she was or where she came from. The farmers called her "the wee fell yin" which is Scots for "the little terror."

Every farmer would have liked to keep her, but as soon as her work was done, she was off and away like a fairy dog.

But one day Wylie went to walk with her masters, and they happened to meet some of the sheep farmers. The farmers stopped and stared at Wylie.

"Why, that's the dog! That's the wee fell yin!" they said. And so it was.

www.summerbridgeactivities.com   Reading Connection—Grade 5—RBP0202

Uncovering Ideas

1. Describe what Wylie looked like.

   _____

   _____

   _____

2. What strange thing did Wylie do when she moved to the city?

   _____

   _____

   _____

3. What name did the farmers give to Wylie?

   _____

   _____

   _____

Connecting to Life

1. Think of a dog that you've known, or one you've seen on a movie or TV. Compare that dog with Wylie.

Wylie   *Another Dog*

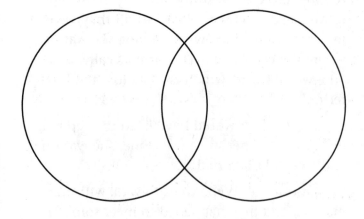

Reading Skills Builder

Compound words are two words joined together to create a different word. An example of a compound word is the word *sawdust*.

Draw lines between the following words to create compound words.

1.	sheep	box
2.	rain	berg
3.	sun	storm
4.	silk	pit
5.	ice	dog
6.	mail	light
7.	arm	land
8.	farm	worm

Word Work

Couch Potato • Counterrevolution

Use your Dictionary

couch potato n: one who spends a great deal of time in front of the television

cougar \'kü-ger\ n. a large, powerful, tawny brown wild American cat

coulee \'kü-lē\ 1. a small stream. 2. a dry streambed. 3. a gully

count \'kount\ vb. to recite numbers in order

1. What are the guide words for this section in the dictionary?

   _____

2. What part of speech is *couch potato*—a noun, verb, adjective, or adverb?

   _____

3. How many different definitions of *coulee* are there? _____

4. How many syllables are in the word *cougar*? _____

The White Heron

By Sarah Orne Jewett, *adapted*

What could you see if you had a bird's view of the world?

Half a mile from home, at the edge of the woods, where the land was highest, a great pine tree stood, the last of its generation. The old pine towered above all and made a landmark for sea and shore miles and miles away. Sylvia knew it well. She had always believed that whoever climbed to the top of it could see the ocean; and the little girl had often laid her hand on the great rough trunk and looked up at those dark boughs. Now she thought of the tree with a new excitement and wondered if by climbing it she could see all the world, and so easily discover where the white heron flew and find the hidden nest.

The thought was almost too real and too great for her childish heart to bear.

All night the door of the little house stood open, and the whippoorwill birds came and sang. Everyone was sound asleep, but Sylvia's great plan kept her awake and watching. She forgot to think of sleep. The short summer night seemed as long as the winter darkness, and at last she crept out of the house and followed the pasture path through the woods, rushing toward the ground beyond, listening to the sleepy chirp of a half-awakened bird.

There was the huge tree asleep in the moonlight, and small and hopeful, Sylvia bravely climbed, with her bare feet and fingers that pinched and held like bird claws to a ladder reaching up, up, almost to the sky. Sylvia felt her way easily.

The tree seemed to reach farther and farther upward as she climbed.

Sylvia's face was like a pale star as she stood shaky and tired high in the treetop. Yes, there was the sea with the dawning sun making a golden dazzle over it, and toward the east flew two hawks. Their gray feathers were as soft as moths; they seemed only a little way from the tree, and Sylvia felt as if she too could go flying away among the clouds. Westward, the woodlands and farms reached miles and miles into the distance; here and there were church steeples, and white villages; truly it was a huge and awesome world.

The birds sang louder and louder. At last the sun came up bewilderingly bright. Sylvia could see the white sails of ships out at sea, and the clouds that had been purple and rose-colored and yellow at first began to fade away. Where was the white heron's nest in the sea of green branches? Now look down again, Sylvia, where the green marsh is; there where you saw the white heron once, you will see him again; look, look! A white spot of him like a single floating feather rises, and goes by the pine tree with a sweep of wing and an outstretched slender neck and crested head. And wait! wait! Do not move a foot or a finger, little girl, for the heron has perched on a pine branch not far from you, and cries back to his mate on the nest, and shakes his feathers for the new day!

The child gives a long sigh. She knows the bird's secret now, the wild, light, slender bird that floats and wavers, and goes back like an arrow to his home in the green world beneath.

www.summerbridgeactivities.com   Reading Connection—Grade 5—RBP0202

Uncovering Ideas

1. Why did Sylvia sneak out of her house?

   _____

   _____

2. What did Sylvia see when she reached the top of the tree?

   ____ a tall mountain with green pines

   ____ a baby squirrel

   ____ the sea

   ____ her house down below

3. From the story, write a description of a setting (place) or an action.

   _____

   _____

   _____

4. From what you've read, describe the character Sylvia.

   _____

   _____

   _____

   _____

Reading Skills Builder

Below is information from a CD by The Electric Eels. Read it and answer the questions below.

This song was inspired by my family's move from Montana to Wyoming.

Rock Springs Blues
  Brig Henry—drums; Ruby Jones—singer; Donald Fender—guitar

My friends and I love to go mountain biking in the hills behind our home. This song came from a day when it started to rain on our ride.

Don't Rain on My Gatorade
  Emie Bailey—African flute; Sean Dees—lead singer; Suzette Hall—banjo

This song is dedicated to my best friend Dylan, who can't eat pizza unless it's so full of cheese you can't see the other toppings.

Extra Cheese, Please
  Truman Foster—mouth harp; Freddy Red—lead singer; Bob Flint—drums

1. What experience inspired the Eels to write "Don't Rain on my Gatorade"?

   _____

   _____

2. Who plays drums on "Extra Cheese, Please"?

   _____

3. Why was "Rock Springs Blues" written?

   _____

   _____

4. What does Emie Bailey play in "Don't Rain on my Gatorade"?

   _____

Word Work

The words below are verbs. Decide which verb goes in which sentence.

listened	rushed	ate	flew	climbed

1. The bird _____ in the sky.
2. Sylvia _____ the tree.
3. The girl _____ to the wind howl.
4. The waves _____ to the shore.
5. The boy _____ his food quickly.

Winter Is a White Owl

By Alisha Golden

What would you compare winter to?

The owl's eyes shine darkly,

As the quiet moon at midnight.

So chillingly cold,

So dark and black.

The snow falls gently,

Like the downy feathers

Of the night watcher.

He floats from tree to limb,

Ever watchful,

In the frosty winter night.

The moon casts her pale light

On the soft snow.

Nature is in silent slumber,

Deeply buried

Under a blanket of white crystals.

The owl is alone,

Except for the moon.

All is still.

www.summerbridgeactivities.com

Uncovering Ideas

1. What images or pictures do you see in your mind as you read this poem?

   _____

   _____

2. Describe the setting of this poem.

   _____

   _____

3. How does the snow fall?

   _____

   _____

4. What is the mood of this poem?

   _____

   _____

Connecting to Life

1. Have you ever been in a forest during the winter? Pick five words to describe what the experience was like.

   _____

   _____

2. How is the world different at night than it is during the day? Using the diagram below, contrast the differences.

Night   *Day*

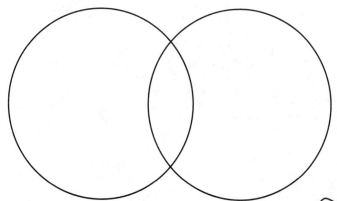

Reading Skills Builder

You want to learn more about identifying animal tracks you see in the woods. After searching the Internet, you come up with this list of sites. Use them to answer the questions below.

1. Commonly seen tracks: fox, squirrel, deer
   www.trailtrecking.com

2. The following might be helpful to anyone interested in identifying cat tracks ...
   www.cattracks.org

3. February's Nature Report. This month you can identify some animal tracks. ...
   www.jonesfarm.com

4. Track the legendary Bigfoot ...
   www.bigfoot.org

   1. Where could you learn how to track cats?

      _____

   2. Which site might show you how to make a cast of an animal track?

      _____

   3. What's the website address where you can find Bigfoot information?

      _____

   4. The first website lists what animals?

      _____

Word Work

The prefix **anti-** means "against." Find six words that have the prefix **anti-** at the beginning. Use your dictionary if you need to.

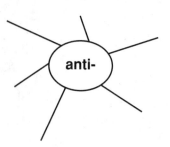

Reading Connection—Grade 5—RBP0202   www.summerbridgeactivities.com   ©RBP Books

The Disappearing Island

By Joseph Soderborg

What if the place where you lived was slowly disappearing?

Nauru is a tiny island about 26 miles south of the equator. It is one of the world's smallest republics, and for the last 100 years is has been slowly shrinking. You might think that rising ocean levels are eroding the island, but people are to blame. Only about 10,000 people live on Nauru. However, most of them make a living by digging up the ground under their feet and selling it. The soil contains rich minerals called phosphates. For nearly a hundred years people have mined the phosphates to sell as fertilizer. The source of the phosphates is birds (or, more specifically, bird droppings).

Seabirds have nested on Nauru for thousands of years, and they covered the entire island with deep deposits of bird droppings. The native population did not seem to mind. The rich soil made it easy for them to grow food, and the sea provided all the fish they needed. It was a peaceful place, far away from civilization. In 1798, the island was "discovered" by a British sea captain named John Fearn. He never set foot on the island, but he called it Pleasant Island because it looked like a tropical paradise covered with trees, and flowers. The island was "claimed" by Germany in 1888. A few years later, a British company discovered the huge phosphate deposits and made a deal with the Germans to start mining. In some places, the deposits were 50 feet deep.

During Word War I, Australia took control of the island. They lost it during World War II.

After the war, Australia, New Zealand, and Great Britain managed the island. The tiny island gained independence in 1968 and took the name Nauru (pronounced Na-oro).

Even after independence, companies continued to strip away the soil and sell it. As a result, the Nauruan people are the richest (per capita) of any Pacific island. But there is a problem. The coral island is only 4 miles long and 2 miles wide, and the phosphates are running out fast. The island is no longer a tropical paradise. Only a thin ring of soil surrounds a wasteland of barren rock. Nauru imports almost everything, including food and drinking water. Nauru exports nothing but phosphates. If the mining slows down, it could mean disaster for the economy. On the other hand, if people continue to mine phosphates, the island just might disappear.

Great Britain, New Zealand, and Australia have agreed to pay $100 million for damage caused by mining. This will help the people for awhile. But without a permanent solution, the island will keep disappearing under the Nauruans' feet.

THERE WAS AN ISLAND HERE A MINUTE AGO...

NAURU ISLAND

Uncovering Ideas

1. What do you think will happen to the people of the island? Why?

_____

_____

2. Think about the island when Captain Fearn saw it. What is it like there? Would you want to live there? Why?

_____

_____

3. How many countries have dug up Nauru to use its rich resources?

_____

_____

4. How is Nauru disappearing?

____ by magic

____ the sea is washing it away

____ people are digging it up and selling it

____ it is being swallowed by a volcano

Connecting to Life

1. If the island is really disappearing, won't the people have to move to another place? Have you ever moved? What is the best thing about moving? What's the worst thing?

_____

_____

_____

Readings Skills Builder

Below is Nauru's national anthem. Read it and answer the questions.

Nauru's National Anthem

Nauru our homeland, the land we dearly love. We all pray for you and we also praise your name. Since long ago you have been the home of our great forefathers, and will be for generations yet to come, We all join in together and say Nauru forevermore.

1. What are two things the anthem says the people will do for Nauru?

_____

_____

2. Write three words that describe how the people of Nauru feel about their island.

_____

_____

Word Work

Nauru Word Search

Word Bank

barren
disaster
industry
nutrient
per capita
phosphates
republic
survival
tropical
wasteland

```
s v a j q j r g n f a c g v
r e p u b l i c r q b z g z
s l h z z m u v c l e d n b
e g g a m b a r r e n i a s
t i p k b i c k p f g s t a
a y r t s u d n i g y a i h
h a d n a l e t s a w s p p
p j u e q l f h u y e t a f
s l a c i p o r t r o e c d
o m t n e i r t u n x r r d
h z a j b f z l o j v i e h
p j y n e s z x z s k n p x
s o b l m i e v w z s e a r
r w w c o s u r v i v a l y
```

Reading Connection—Grade 5—RBP0202   www.summerbridgeactivities.com   ©RBP Books

Shirley Temple: America's Little Princess

By Alisha Golden

Have you ever dreamed of being "discovered"?

In the 1930s, Shirley Temple was the biggest little star in the world. Her movies helped people forget hard times during the Great Depression. She lifted spirits with her dimpled smile and trademark bouncy curls. President Franklin D. Roosevelt once said: "It's a splendid thing that for just fifteen cents, an American can go to a movie and look at the smiling face of a baby and forget his troubles. As long as we have Shirley Temple, we will be all right."

When she was born on April 23, 1928, in California, no one suspected what was in store for Shirley Jane Temple. It all started one Thanksgiving after a tap lesson. At the age of three, she was "discovered" by a young movie director and his assistant. From there she soon progressed to movie stardom. Every day in front of the camera, her mother would tell her, "Sparkle Shirley, sparkle." And she did. She made nine movies in 1934 and won a special "Oscar" award. Shirley was the box-office champ for three straight years, 1936,1937, and 1938. She beat out great grown-up stars like Clark Gable, Bing Crosby, Gary Cooper, and Joan Crawford.

Shirley had a more normal life as a teenager. She went to an all-girls high school and enjoyed sodas, sock hops, and even schoolwork. But as Shirley grew older, her movies were less popular at the box office. So she gracefully retired from acting. Not long afterward, on a trip to Hawaii, she met the love of her life, Charles Black. They married in 1950. Shirley enjoyed almost fifty years and two children with "Charley."

Almost two decades later, Shirley Temple Black was back in the spotlight. She announced that she was running for the U.S. Congress. She lost the election, but she went on to enjoy a long, successful career with the United Nations and the State Department. She was an ambassador to the United Nations, Ghana, and Czechoslovakia. A battle with cancer only made the public admire her more. She won that battle and told her story to give others hope.

A friend of hers once said, "[Her mother's] wish was that Shirley would grow into a woman of character, faith, and usefulness." There is no question that she did.

Uncovering Ideas

1. How old was Shirley Temple when she was "discovered"?

   _____

2. Why do you think Shirley Temple was so popular?

   _____

   _____

   _____

3. How much did a movie cost during the Great Depression?

   ____ $1.00

   ____ 75 cents

   ____ a dime

   ____ 15 cents

Connecting to Life

1. Sometimes people go to movies to escape reality. Can you think of some movies that are not realistic and some that are like real life? Which kinds of movies do you like best?

Write at least three movies under each column:

Realistic	Not realistic
_____	_____
_____	_____
_____	_____

2. Who is your favorite actor or actress? Why do you like this person?

   _____

   _____

3. On a separate sheet of paper, write a letter to the actor or actress, telling him or her about yourself.

Reading Skills Builder

Be a newspaper reporter and fill in the blanks with the correct word or phrase.

_____ was a famous
(who)

actress. She was born in _____. She
(where)

was discovered while _____.
(what)

She was married to _____.
(who)
Throughout her life,

people admired her because _____
(why)

_____.

Word Work

Shirley Temple Word Search

```
m k s c a n d i d a c y q s x
w x j q t s s c i a s f t u t
s w w h h i n z n m s v k m d
a b x o g g o f o i e y r u c
s r d a m j i w i u n k a y f
u u t q j x t n p q e b m k l
a n w l b e a a m e r o e h e
i x w v y i n i a y a x d x t
z h c g a c d f h y w o a y e
l o v y a d e t c g a f r z n
q c q r o e t g p b m f t h a
q a e b h q i k o y a i y q c
t e k f a c n c t b k c y h i
r p o w a z u r j k t e j x t
q j s p o p u l a r i t y v v
```

Word Bank

box office	candidacy	popularity
trademark	United Nations	champion
career	awareness	tenacity

www.summerbridgeactivities.com

The Man Who Would Not Die

By Joseph Soderborg

What would it be like to be forgotten on a battlefield?

William Brown was one of the luckiest soldiers in the American Civil War. He served in the Eighteenth Iowa infantry. Iowans were known for the sacrifices they made to protect the Union. In fact, the men and women from Iowa did more than their share. The state had a higher percentage of its men serving in the Union army than any other state. About 43 percent of military-aged men served in one of the many regiments raised there. One of them was William Brown, a farmer who nearly died from wounds he got in a battle in Cow Creek, Kansas.

A band of Confederate guerrillas and William's company bumped into each other at Cow Creek and started shooting. It wasn't even much of a battle, but for William, it proved to be the battle of his life.

The two sides skirmished for a bit; some were killed and some wounded. William was among the wounded. Somehow he had stepped into a hailstorm of enemy bullets. Maybe he was exposed during a pause when there was nobody else to shoot at except him. He was shot so many times, nobody thought he had survived. But he wasn't dead!

Young William began an excruciating struggle for his life. He lay on the battleground semi-conscious, exposed to the heat of the day and the frosty nights. He had nothing to eat or drink. He could have given up, but he knew that meant death, so he hung on. Thousands of soldiers in the war died from minor wounds that simply became infected. William had fifteen wounds, had broken his arm, and had lost a lot of blood. It was five days before he was rescued and nursed back to health. His will to live was stronger than the one pound of lead that had entered his body.

After the war, William became a farmer, but he did not live completely happily ever after. He limped and endured pain for the rest of his life. He had many trials and had to apply for help from the government because of his disabilities. He suffered mental illness and fatigue, but despite all that, he married and raised a family. William Brown was a hero and a living testament of the will to survive. He is significant because he represents the sacrifices made by all those from the great state of Iowa. But he also symbolizes the nation as a whole, which refused to die even as it suffered from its own war wounds for many years after a horrible war.

Uncovering Ideas

1. What reason does the author give for William getting wounded so badly?

   _____

   _____

2. Why do you think William joined the army?

   _____

   _____

3. The author compares William Brown to the nation. What were some of the nation's wounds after the Civil War? What does war do to a country?

   _____

   _____

   _____

   _____

4. Was William Brown lucky because he survived or unlucky because he got hurt so badly in the first place?

   _____

   _____

Connecting to Life

It wasn't just soldiers who made sacrifices during the Civil War. Regular citizens made sacrifices, too. What do you think some of these sacrifices were? Do soldiers and their families make similar sacrifices today?

_____

_____

_____

Reading Skills Builder

Redundant words are words that mean the same thing and don't need to be together. Cross out the unneeded word:

a strong bodybuilder

the natural outdoors

peace and tranquility

excellent goodness

a fiesta party

a big giant

happy celebration

mystery of the unknown

Word Work

Write two **antonyms** for each of the following words. Antonyms are words with opposite meanings.

serve _____ _____

learn _____ _____

expose _____ _____

Use each word and one of its antonyms in a sentence. Have each sentence contain exactly 13 words.

_____

_____

_____

_____

_____

_____

_____

_____

_____

World's Biggest Cat and Other Guinness World Record Holders Celebrate Downtown

By Howard Jukes, Entertainment Reporter for the *Park Valley Times*

Why would anybody eat a fork?

Local hairdresser Emma Jo Hall noticed something strange on her way to work this morning. On her route through Clyde Park, she passed a man balancing a bottle of milk on his head, two hairy-faced gentlemen, a 35-pound cat, and a French guy who was eating a metal fork.

"I wondered what planet I was on," said the confused Ms. Hall.

Hall hadn't been transported to some unknown planet. She found herself among dozens of record breakers from the Guinness Book of World Records at a party held Thursday and Friday at Clyde Park. The party celebrates the feats of record holders. The city hopes it will draw a big enough crowd to become the largest party the state has ever seen.

A 6,000-foot banana cake spanned the waterfront by the park. Local bakers had been busy mixing huge amounts of batter to create a replica of the longest cake ever made. The cake at Clyde Park missed the mark by 2,000 feet. The original cake, created by chefs from Dubai in the United Arab Emirates on December 2, 1996, was 8,303 feet long.

Strangest Diet

Michel Lotito turned down a bite of the party cake because he said bananas make him sick. He decided to eat his fork instead. Michel, from Grenoble, France, has a thing for metal; he eats it. Michel has been eating metal and glass since 1959. He can eat two pounds of metal per day.

Largest Underwater Wedding

Susan Carroll and Scott Hamblen walked around wearing flippers and wet suits. The couple holds the world's record for being married in the largest underwater wedding ceremony. It took place on April 12, 2001. Thirty-nine certified divers remained submerged in the Florida Keys National Marine Sanctuary for the ten-minute wedding.

Most Records

One of the party-goers was Ashrita Furman from Brooklyn, New York. He has broken 14 records in his life, giving him another record: the person who holds the most world records. He broke his first record in 1979 by doing 27,000 jumping jacks. When Ashrita was young, he wasn't good at sports. Now Ashrita holds the record for the most hopscotch games in 24 hours (434 games), the most rope jumps in 24 hours (130,000), and the fastest 10-km sack race (1 hour, 25 minutes, 10 seconds). Other records he holds include the most underwater rope jumps in one hour (738), and the fastest pogo stick ascent of Canada's CN Tower (57 minutes, 51 seconds). Watch out for this guy; who knows what he'll try next. Ashrita even holds the record for the greatest distance walked while balancing a milk bottle on his head (80.96 miles in 1998). It took him 23 hours, 35 minutes to finish his walk. "I don't even have a flat head," says Ashrita.

www.summerbridgeactivities.com
Reading Connection—Grade 5—RBP0202

Uncovering Ideas

1. If you could meet one of the record holders from this story, who would you meet? Write three questions you would ask them.

   _____

   _____

   _____

2. Fill in the information from the story:

   a. The longest cake in the world was_____ feet long and was made in _____.

   b. _____ broke his first world record by doing 27,000 _____.

   c. The largest underwater _____ took place when _____ married_____. There were _____ certified divers, all submerged in the Florida Keys National _____ _____.

3. What do you think is the most interesting thing that Ashrita Furman did to break a world's record?

   _____

Connecting to Life

1. If you could break any world record, which would it be, and how would you break it?

   _____

   _____

2. Write an invitation trying to get your friends to attend the World Records Party. Make it exciting to catch their attention.

   _____

   _____

Reading Skills Builder

Read this passage from a dictionary page, and answer the questions below.

museum (myoo ze' em) n. A building in which objects of artistic, historical, or scientific interest are exhibited.

mush 1. (mush) n. 1. A porridge made of cornmeal boiled in water or milk. 2. A soft, thick mass. 3. Extreme sentimentality: That movie was just a lot of mush.

mush 2. To travel over snow with a dog sled —interjection. An expression used to command a team of sled dogs to start pulling or to go faster.

1. What kinds of objects does the definition of *museum* say are found in a museum?

   _____

2. Looking at the definition of museum, what do you think the word *exhibited* means?

   _____

3. In the following sentences, write which definition of *mush* goes with each.

   a. The movie about the girl and the boy falling in love was all a bunch of mush. Definition: _____

   b. "Do we have to eat mush again today?" Definition: _____

   c. The man yelled "mush!" to the dogs. Definition: _____

Word Work

Under each **word part**, write down three words that have that word part at the beginning. Then write down the definition of each word.

re—definition: back or again
   return—to give back

   _____

   _____

ex—definition: out _____

   _____

   _____

auto—definition: self _____

   _____

   _____

World's Biggest Cat and Other Guinness Record Holders Celebrate Downtown

By Howard Jukes, Entertainment Reporter for the *Park Valley Times*

Have you ever seen a five-mile-long gum wrapper chain?

Biggest Cat

On Thursday at the park, Frieda Ireland was telling local kids that it was okay to pet her famous 35-pound cat, Leo. Leo, a Maine Coon cat, is as long as an eight-year-old child. "We have to keep our eye on him when we're cooking," says owner Frieda. "He can stand up and put his paws on the kitchen counter." But Leo's not after the food. "He enjoys sweeping things off the counter, not eating them!"

Longest Chain Made from Gum Wrappers

Have you ever made a gum wrapper chain? You ought to take lessons from Gary Duschl, of Ontario, Canada, who has been making a gum wrapper chain since March 11, 1965. Gary sat in a corner of Clyde Park with his massive 466-pound creation. The chain currently measures 34,077 feet and is made up of 1,585,382 links from 792,691 wrappers.

Longest Hair

Another attraction at the event was Hoo Sateow's hair. In 1997, his hair, at 16 feet 11 inches long, was the longest in the world. Hoo stopped cutting his hair when he was 18 years old. Earlier that year, he'd cut his hair and had gotten sick, so he decided not to cut it again. Hoo is a medicine man who likes to weave his hair into a beehive under a hat.

Other record breakers you can catch at the Clyde Park Party include:

Most Clothespins Clipped on Face

Garry Turner's claim to fame came when he to clipped 133 wooden clothespins onto his face in London, on August 3, 2001.

Most Couples Kissing Simultaneously

Other record breakers attending included couples who helped break the record for the most people kissing simultaneously. The record was broken by 1,588 pairs in Sarnia, Ontario, Canada, on February 11, 2000. Couples had to keep their lips locked for 10 seconds for the record to count.

Longest Time Trapped in an Elevator

Kiveli Papajohn was trapped in a small elevator for six days. She kept alive by eating bits of a few tomatoes she had with her.

Longest Fingernails

Shridhar Chillal of Poona, India, may give you his right hand to shake, which looks normal enough. But the nails on his left hand measure a combined length of 20 feet 2.25 inches. As a boy, he had wanted to do something outstanding, so he chose to grow his nails. Growing his fingernails to that length has been a difficult thing. He's had to do all his daily tasks with his right hand and has given up many good nights of sleep.

Youngest Billionaire

Yahoo! is the website that made Jerry Yang (USA), the co-founder of Yahoo! Inc., a billionaire in 1998. This made Jerry the youngest billionaire in the world at age 29. He is now worth about $4 billion.

(The party in this story is fictional, but the people and records are real. For more information about World Record holders, visit www.guinnessworldrecords.com.)

83

Uncovering Ideas

1. If you wanted to be a part of the record for the most people kissing simultaneously, where would you have had to go?

   _____

2. What does Leo's owner have to watch out for when Leo's in the kitchen?

   _____

   _____

3. List three reasons why you think these people may have decided to break a world record.

   _____

   _____

   _____

Connecting to Life

1. This story talks about people that have done things no one else has ever done. What are things that you do, or someone you know does, that no one else does?

   _____

   _____

2. If you could become famous by doing something strange, would you do it? Write a short article about how you broke a world record by doing something unusual.

   _____

   _____

   _____

   _____

   _____

Reading Skills Builder

In the blanks below, write whether the sentence is stating a fact or an opinion.

1. The largest underwater wedding was held in Florida. _____

2. Weddings are boring. _____

3. Most people have hair. _____

4. Pink is the best color. _____

5. Everyone likes holidays. _____

6. Jerry Yang is the co-founder of Yahoo!

   _____

7. Big cats are better than small cats.

   _____

8. Pink is the name of a color. _____

9. The man won the award for the longest hair. _____

10. School lunch is very good.

    _____

11. My teacher will give a test tomorrow.

    _____

Word Work

Find words that are the opposite of the following words. Use your dictionary if necessary.

1. *Different* is the opposite of _____

2. *Summer* is the opposite of _____

3. *Nervous* is the opposite of _____

4. *Tired* is the opposite of _____

5. *Love* is the opposite of _____

6. *Waking* if the opposite of _____

7. *Play* is the opposite of _____

8. *Clumsy* is the opposite of _____

9. *Impatient* is the opposite of _____

10. *Grouchy* is the opposite of _____

Reading Connection—Grade 5—RBP0202   www.summerbridgeactivities.com   ©RBP Books

Answer Pages

Page 6

Uncovering Ideas
1. Pouring in cupfuls of hot water.
2. Answers will vary.

Connecting to Life
1. Answers will vary.
2. Answers will vary.
3. Answers will vary.

Reading Skills Builder
1. C/F
2. A
3. B/G
4. F
5. E
6. B/G
7. F
8. D

Word Work
1. Answers will vary.
2. Answers will vary.

Page 8

Uncovering Ideas
1. Answers will vary.
2. Answers will vary.
3. Answers will vary.
4. Answers will vary.

Reading Skills Builder
1. Answers will vary.
2. Answers will vary.
3. Answers will vary.
4. Answers will vary.
5. Answers will vary.

Word Work
1. like a cat
2. over the harbor and city
3. moves on
4. a cat

Page 10

Uncovering Ideas
1. The land is below sea level. The wall keeps the ocean out.
2. He put his finger in the hole to keep the water from breaking the dike.
3. He told his brother to run for help.

Connecting to Life
1. Answers will vary.

Reading Skills Builder
1. attend the art show, street dance, fireworks, or rodeo
2. The Stanley City Council www.moonbeamfilmsidaho.com

Word Work
Answers will vary.

Page 12

Uncovering Ideas
1. Answers will vary.
   A small act can make a huge difference.
2. Answers will vary.

Connecting to Life
1. Answers will vary.
2. Answers will vary.

Reading Skills Builder
1. treasure hunt
   offer to baby-sit her cat
   pretend you are sick
2. cover a mug in tinfoil
3. Answers will vary.

Word Work
1. Answers will vary.
2. Answers will vary.
3. Answers will vary.
4. Answers will vary.

Answer Pages

Page 14

Uncovering Ideas
1. Jess and her brother are wading up a river to a waterfall.
2. Answers will vary.
3. Jess. c.
4. Answers will vary. She was a tomboy.

Connecting to Life
1-2. Answers will vary.

Reading Skills Builder
Answers will vary.

Word Work
1. The actor did a great job playing the groom of a monster.
2. The king's daughter is the heroine of the story.
3. My niece asked me to read her a story about the Prince and the Pea.
4. The waitress took the meal to the hungry woman.
5. The old woman went searching for the ewe.

Page 16

Uncovering Ideas
1. Answers will vary.

Jess hikes to Jim.	They rest on a rock.	Jim encourages Jess and hikes on to the water-fall.	Jim falls.

Connecting to Life
1-2. Answers will vary.

Reading Skills Builder
1. Section B—Get Well
2. Section C—Weddings
3. Section D—Fourth of July

Word Work
1. there
2. They're
3. their

Page 18

Uncovering Ideas
1. Answers will vary. She helped him from the river; she went for help.
2. b.
3. Answers will vary.

Connecting to Life
1. Answers will vary.

Word Work
1. butterfly
2. garbage
3. before
4. nephew
5. chain
6. scared
7. butter
8. chicken

Reading Skills Builder
1. Popsicle sticks, glue, glue gun, paint, markers, photo. Answers will vary.
2. Attach a ribbon; hang the photo.
3. Answers will vary.

Page 20

Uncovering Ideas
1. Answers will vary. You have to depend on others' accounts.
2. History is subject to interpretation.
3. Answers will vary.
4. Answers will vary.

Connecting to Life
1-2. Answers will vary.

Reading Skills Builder
1. footsteps
2. a potato, a needle, a storm
3. a chimney
4. the moon
5. an onion
6. a secret

Word Work
1. choir
2. Christmas
3. chlorine
4. mechanic
5. characters

Reading Connection—Grade 5—RBP0202   www.summerbridgeactivities.com   © RBP Books

Answer Pages

Page 22

Uncovering Ideas
1. Answers will vary. Americans were worried that immigrants would take jobs or cause trouble.
2. An earthquake; citizenship records were destroyed.
3. It kept Chinese immigrants from coming to America.

Connecting to Life
1. Answers will vary.
2. Answers will vary.

Reading Skills Builder
3, 2, 5, 4, 1

Word Work

Page 24

Uncovering Ideas
1. Answers will vary.
2. Answers will vary. The writer is far from home in a strange environment, like a fish out of water.
3. Answers will vary. Their families, food, money, freedom.

Connecting to Life
1. Answers will vary. 2. Answers will vary.

Reading Skills Builder
Answers will vary.
Dog Walker. 2 yrs. exp. teaching dog obedience. Lg. or sm. dogs. $10 p/hr. per dog. Kyle Jones (D) 466-4883 (E) 473-3221

Word Work
1. detained
2. unbearable
3. ideal
4. restriction
5. scarcity
6. ambition
7. humility

Page 26

Uncovering Ideas
1. She was a tomboy.
2. b.
3. I love to dance!

Connecting to Life
1. Answers will vary.
2. Answers will vary.

Reading Skills Builder
Answers will vary.

Word Work
1. wonderful
2. powerful
3. helpful
4. handful
5. mouthful
6. graceful
7. dreadful
8. careful

1. careful
2. handful
3. graceful
4. helpful
5. mouthful

Page 28

Uncovering Ideas
1. The British soldiers are fighting the Hillsmen. The soldiers come from England, and the Hillsmen come from India.
2. Answers will vary.
3. It refers to the red thread the Hillsmen tied around the wrist to honor brave warriors.

Connecting to Life
1. Answers will vary.

Reading Skills Builder
1. celebrate
2. happy
3. chill
4. classic
5. fast
6. couple
7. deform

Word Work
1. barricade
2. ravine
3. precipice

© RBP Books   www.summerbridgeactivities.com   Reading Connection—Grade 5—RBP0202

Page 30

Uncovering Ideas
1. Russia.
2. Answers will vary: Russia, Sweden, USA, Swaziland, Argentina, Turkey, Uzbekistan, Japan, California, Texas, North Carolina, Tokyo, San Francisco, Houston, Portland.
3. Because in 2003 the space shuttle *Columbia* crashed.

Connecting to Life
1-2. Answers will vary.

Reading Skills Builder
1. E
2. F
3. D
4. Answers will vary.
5. Answers will vary.

Word Work
1. Answers will vary.

Page 32

Uncovering Ideas
1. The rice fields provided the people's food.
2. To warn the people of the tidal wave
3. Answers will vary. Many people would have drowned.

Connecting to Life
1. Answers will vary.

Reading Skills Builder
1. A
2. D
3. Answers will vary. Upset.
4. To Pocatello, Idaho.

Word Work
1. potato field
2. patient
3. tank
4. gloves, mittens
5. water

Page 34

Uncovering Ideas
1. C
2. Answers will vary. She died.
3. Answers will vary.

Connecting to Life
1. Answers will vary.

Reading Skills Builder
5, 1, 6, 2, 3, 4

Word Work
A. 11, 7, 10, 8
B. Answers will vary.
C. king / dom   2
     bring / ing   2
     ma / ny   2
     mai / den   2
     Ann / a / bel   3
     dreams   1
     dis / sev / er   3

Page 36

Uncovering Ideas
1-3. Answers will vary.

Connecting to Life
1. Answers will vary.

Reading Skills Builder
1. 1, 2, 3, 5, 4

Word Work
1. a march
2. hill
3. to eat up
4. to begin
5. setting

Answer Pages

Page 38

Uncovering Ideas
1. Answers will vary.
2. springtime
3. C
4. because the stone was cold

Connecting to Life
1. Answers will vary.
2. Answers will vary: to explain the coloration on a bird's wings.
3. Answers will vary.

Reading Skills Builder
4, 6, 2, 5, 1, 3

Word Work
1. brightly
2. happily
3. carefully
4. quickly
5. awfully
6. sweetly
7. loudly
8. wildly
9. quietly
10. wonderfully

Page 40

Uncovering Ideas
1. Timeline could include the following events: Born 1857, goes to school until fourth grade, printer's apprentice, candy maker's apprentice, age 18 opens candy shop in Philadelphia, at 24 moves to Denver, learns to make caramels, 1886 moves to Lancaster, 1893 gets idea for making chocolate, 1894 establishes Hershey Chocolate Company, marries, 1900 sells company, 1909 opens the Milton Hershey School, 1945 dies
2. He got the idea after seeing chocolate making equipment at the Chicago International Exposition.
3. Answers will vary.

Connecting to Life
1. Answers will vary.

Reading Skills Builder
1. abnormal
2. enjoying life
3. easy to please
4. holy cow
5. I'm the one for you
6. I accelerate

Word Work
1. accompanied
2. worried
3. cities
4. buried
5. luxurious
6. emergencies

Page 42

Uncovering Ideas
1. how even farm animals can become pets
2. Answers will vary: because they have become friends with their animals.
3. Wild Thing   Buckey J. McKay
   Big Red   Adam Swann
   Wilber   Shauna Jepsen
   Dusty   Christie Owen
4. Answers will vary.

Connecting to Life
1. Answers will vary.

Reading Skills Builder
1. bowlegged: legs that bow out at the knee
2. bull: a male cow
3. Jersey: a breed of dairy cow
4. lasso: a leather rope
5. bridle: headgear used to control a horse

Word Work
1. H/K
2. B
3. E
4. H/K
5. I
6. F
7. G
8. L
9. A
10. J
11. C
12. D

Page 44

Uncovering Ideas
1. Answers will vary.
2. She was a social worker
3. Answers will vary. The public liked her: they thought she was witty, charming, and intelligent. They called her Lady Lindy.

Connecting to Life
1. Answers will vary.
2. Answers will vary.

Reading Skills Builder
1. 7 miles
2. Fruit Loop
3. Right

Word Work

© RBP Books   www.summerbridgeactivities.com   Reading Connection—Grade 5—RBP0202

Page 46

Uncovering Ideas
1. He hit his head and fell into a river. The river took him to a different place.
2. A lamb was licking his face.
3. Answers will vary. He is a friendly shepherd.

Connecting to Life
1-2. Answers will vary.

Reading Skills Builder
The words that should be circled to show TIME are: Yesterday, next day, last week, now, tomorrow, next week.
The words that should be circled that show ORDER are: Before, first, then, next, after that, later, the next day.

Word Work
1. without aim
2. without harm
3. without care
4. without fear
5. c.
6. c.
7. Answers may vary.
8. Answers may vary.
9. Answers may vary.
10. Answers may vary.

Page 48

Uncovering Ideas
1. Answers may vary. A small, sparsely furnished cottage.
2. Answers may vary.

Connecting to Life
1-2. Answers will vary.

Reading Skills Builder
Answers will vary.
Tongue licks Finlay's face. Finlay meets Murchadh. Finlay goes home with Murchadh. Finlay leaves Murchadh's.

Word Work

```
d o y f o o g d t c e m
l v d d c x u e l h d o
e u g n o t r h a t i s
n r l w q q l c d c a s
t h g s h b l a n m l y
g a t z x x i d n c p i
n s n o g z n a o a b v
b k z g r p g e t n d l
y q m t l b j h t v r k
s l o b b e r t u a r v
y m n r n l d p m s l t
s u o i r u f x a k s y
```

Page 50

Uncovering Ideas
1. If you spent the night there a voice would tell you where to find luck.
2. B
3. D

Connecting to Life
1-2. Answers will vary.

Reading Skills Builder
1. 20
2. 5
3. 5
4. 17
5. 12

Word Work
1. The colorful rock fell out of my pocket.
2. It was a cool night.
3. The boy had skinny legs.
4. The old shepherd gave the boy some stew.
5. Please turn off the hot water.
6. He climbed down the tangled branches.
7. The red fox ran through the woods.

Page 52

Uncovering Ideas
1. Answers will vary.
2. Coyotes, rabbits, foxes, lizards. They hide in the day to keep them out of the sun; they try to blend into the land.
3. Answers will vary.

Connecting to Life
1. Answers will vary.

Reading Skills Builder
d. a map of the United States

Word Work
Answers will vary.

Answer Pages

Page 54

Uncovering Ideas
1. b.
2. <u>Asthma</u> — open up nasal passages to help you breathe better
   <u>Dry Skin</u> — soften dry hands
   <u>Arthritis</u> — The bee venom in the bee sting helped the knees and joints to move better.

Connecting to Life
1. Answers will vary.

Reading Skills Builder
1. 30 years
2. the heart of small-town Idaho
3. Answers will vary. It is fresh from the honeycomb and not diluted like other honey.

Word Work

<u>Honey</u>	<u>Bees</u>
dripping	pesky
fresh	noisy
sweet	buzzing
raw	angry

Page 56

Uncovering Ideas
1. Answers will vary: a bird walking, eating a worm, drinking a dew, then flying away.
2. c.

Connecting to Life
1. Answers will vary.

Reading Skills Builder
1. *James and the Giant Peach*—Dahl
2. *Mossflower*—Jacques
3. *The Giver*— Lowry
4. *Hatchet*—Paulsen
5. *The Hobbit*—Tolkien

Word Work
1-3. Answers will vary.

Contractions:
1. you're
2. they're
3. we're
4. isn't
5. weren't
6. aren't

Page 58

Uncovering Ideas
1. Answers will vary.
2. Answers will vary. He was disappointed; he was afraid of what he had created.
3. Before electric lights were invented. "My candle was nearly burnt out."

Connecting to Life
1-2. Answers will vary.

Reading Skills Builder
1. d.

Word Work

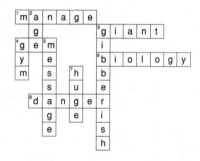

Page 60

Uncovering Ideas
1. Answers will vary.
2. Answers will vary. Depressed, nervous, crazy, afraid, etc.
3. Answers will vary.

Connecting to Life
1. Answers will vary.

Reading Skills Builder
1. wheat bran
2. BHT
3. Emerald City, Kansas
4. nine

Word Work
healthy—sick
happy—sad
friend—enemy
war—peace
in—out
up—down
work—play
cold—hot

Page 62

Uncovering Ideas
1. Borogove
2. c.
3. 'Twas four o'clock (the time to broil things for dinner) and the active, slimy badger/lizard (corkscrew-like) creatures did go round and round and make holes in the grass plot around a sundial.

Connecting to Life
1. Answers will vary.
2. Answers will vary.

Reading Skills Builder
1-5. Answers will vary.

Word Work
Answers will vary.

Page 64

Uncovering Ideas
1. Corps of Discovery
2. Answers will vary.
3. His stories were so fantastic and amazing, they thought his stories were made up.

Connecting to Life
1. Answers will vary.
2. Answers will vary.

Reading Skills Builder
1. 5
2. 4
3. 1
4. 6
5. 3
6. 2

Word Work

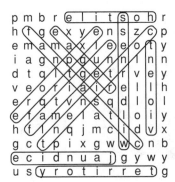

Page 66

Uncovering Ideas
1. Answers will vary: Wyoming; on cactus-covered prairies with sharp volcanic rocks; in the mountains and close to a river.
2. They were planning to kill John Colter.
3. Answers will vary.

Connecting to Life
1. Answers will vary.
2. Answers will vary.

Reading Skills Builder
1. Answers will vary.

Word Work

```
o w s m q r a d i z b s d f
p u y n m d y f x j m n e q
r x v j y e t r c s h i r y
o n w x r l e z h o w s u b
a l b a b t r s o e a t p u
v v p e i r t s t d c p g g
s q u c p d w c e h i c a f
e p y i s e v a d e z o c e
l l p n u r v c s d s m h y
y o n a m c t t p h o u z x
t g q c l b n k u t c h f g
w j i l q i d s g t k p x w
d a y o o y x h e g l b x e
i m l v x p h d c l k e f z
```

Page 68

Uncovering Ideas
1. grass, clover, berries, nuts, ant-eggs, fish, flesh, fowl, honey, (sometimes tree bark and rotten logs)
2. He means that you learn more by spending a day in the mountains than you do by reading a whole cartload of books.
3. Answers will vary.

Connecting to Life
1. Answers will vary.

Reading Skills Builder
1. 1
2. 4
3. 6
4. 7
5. 2
6. 3
7. 5

Word Work
1-3. Answers will vary.

Answer Pages

Page 70

Uncovering Ideas
1. A slim, silky-haired, sharp-eared dog who was the prettiest thing you could imagine.
2. She disappeared every Tuesday night and was back in the morning.
3. The Wee Fell Yin.

Connecting to Life
1. Answers will vary.

Reading Skills Builder
1. sheepdog
2. rainstorm
3. sunlight
4. silkworm
5. iceberg
6. mailbox
7. armpit
8. farmland

Word Work
1. Couch Potato and Counterrevolution
2. Noun
3. Three
4. Two

Page 72

Uncovering Ideas
1. She wanted to climb the tree.
2. the sea
3. Answers will vary.
4. Answers will vary.

Reading Skills Builder
1. a bike ride in the rain with friends
2. Bob Flint
3. because of the writer's move from Montana to Rock Springs
4. the African flute

Word Work
1. flew
2. climbed
3. listened
4. rushed
5. ate

Page 74

Uncovering Ideas
1. Answers will vary.
2. At night in a forest during the winter while the snow is falling.
3. It's gently falling.
4. Answers will vary.

Connecting to Life
1-2. Answers will vary.

Reading Skills Builder
1. www.cattracks.org
2. www.trailtrecking.com, or www.cattracks.org, or www.jonesfarm.com
3. www.bigfoot.org
4. fox, squirrel, and deer

Word Work
1. Answers will vary.

Page 76

Uncovering Ideas
1. Answers will vary.
2. When he saw the island, it looked like a tropical paradise with trees and flowers. (The rest of the answers will vary.)
3. Three: Australia, New Zealand, and Great Britain
4. People are digging it up and selling it.

Connecting to Life
1. Answers will vary.

Reading Skills Builder
1. pray for her, and praise her name
2. Answers will vary.

Word Work

```
s v a j q j r g n f a c g v
r e p u b l i c r q b z g z
s l h z z m u v c l e d n b
e g g a m b a r r e n i a s
t i p k b i c k p f g s t a
a y r t s u d n i g y a i h
h a d n a l e t s a w s p p
p j u e q l f h u y e t a f
s l a c i p o r t r o e c d
o m t n e i r t u n x r r d
h z a j b f z l o j v i e h
p j y n e s z x z s k n p x
s o b l m i e v w z s e a r
r w w c o s u r v i v a l y
```

© RBP Books   www.summerbridgeactivities.com   Reading Connection—Grade 5—RBP0202

Page 78

Uncovering Ideas
1. three years old
2. Answers will vary.
3. 15 cents

Connecting to Life
1-3. Answers will vary.

Reading Skills Builder
Shirley Temple was a famous actress. She was born in *California*. She was discovered *while she was tap-dancing*. She was first married to *Charles Black*. Throughout her life, people admired her because *(answers will vary)*.

Word Work

Page 80

Uncovering Ideas
1. He may have been exposed to the bullets during a pause when there was no one else to shoot at.
2. Answers will vary.
3. Answers will vary.
4. Answers will vary.

Connecting to Life
Answers will vary.

Reading Skills Builder
a ~~strong~~ bodybuilder
the ~~natural~~ outdoors
~~peace~~ and tranquility
~~excellent~~ goodness
a ~~fiesta~~ party
a ~~big~~ giant
~~happy~~ celebration
~~mystery~~ of the unknown

Word Work
Answers will vary.

Page 82

Uncovering Ideas
1. Answers will vary.
2. a. The longest cake in the world was *8,303 feet long* and was made in the *United Arab Emirates*.
   b. *Ashrita Furman* broke his first world record by doing 27,000 *jumping jacks*.
   c. The largest underwater *wedding* took place when *Susan Carroll* married *Scott Hamblen*. There were *39* certified divers all submerged in the Florida Keys *National Marine Sanctuary*.
3. Answers will vary.

Connecting to Life
1-2. Answers will vary.

Reading Skills Builder
1. objects of artistic, historical, or scientific interest
2. Answers will vary: *Exhibit* means to put on show, or to display.
3. a. extreme sentimentality
   b. a porridge made of cornmeal boiled in water or milk
   c. an expression used to command a team of sled dogs

Word Work
Answers will vary.

Page 84

Uncovering Ideas
1. Sarnia, Ontario, Canada.
2. To make sure that Leo doesn't sweep things off the counter.
3. Answers will vary.

Connecting to Life
1-2. Answers will vary.

Reading Skills Builder
1. fact	2. opinion	3. fact
4. opinion	5. opinion	6. fact
7. opinion	8. fact	9. fact
10. opinion	11. fact	

Word Work (Exact words may differ.)
1. same	2. winter	3. calm
4. energetic	5. hate	6. sleeping
7. work	8. graceful	9. patient
10. pleasant, happy		

Reading Connection—Grade 5—RBP0202   www.summerbridgeactivities.com   ©RBP Books

Notes

_____
_____
_____
_____
_____
_____
_____
_____
_____
_____
_____
_____
_____
_____
_____
_____
_____
_____
_____
_____
_____
_____

5 Five things I'm thankful for:

1. _____
2. _____
3. _____
4. _____
5. _____

Notes

Five things I'm thankful for:

1. _____
2. _____
3. _____
4. _____
5. _____